American Indian Educators in Reservation Schools

American Indian Educators in Reservation Schools

TERRY HUFFMAN

UNIVERSITY OF NEVADA PRESS  RENO & LAS VEGAS

University of Nevada Press, Reno, Nevada 89557 USA
Copyright © 2013 by University of Nevada Press
All rights reserved
Manufactured in the United States of America

Library of Congress Cataloging-in-Publication Data

Huffman, Terry E., 1958–
 American Indian educators in reservation schools /
Terry Huffman.
 p. cm.
Includes bibliographical references and index.
ISBN 978-0-87417-907-1 (cloth : alk. paper) —
ISBN 978-0-87417-908-8 (ebook)
 1. Indian teachers—United States. 2. Indian students—
United States. 3. Indian reservations—United States.
4. Indians of North America—Education. I. Title.
E97.H783 2013
371.8297—dc23   2012037303

The paper used in this book meets the requirements of
American National Standard for Information Sciences—
Permanence of Paper for Printed Library Materials, ANSI/
NISO Z39.48-1992 (R2002). Binding materials were selected
for strength and durability.

University of Nevada Press Paperback Edition, 2014
22 21 20 19 18 17 16 15 14
5 4 3 2 1

ISBN-13: 978-0-87417-946-0 (pbk.: alk. paper)

To the twenty-one who shared their stories of hope

Contents

Preface ix

Introduction   1

1. Hope for a Better Tomorrow
 Affinitive Educators and Facilitative Educators   11

2. Every Reason to Succeed
 Characteristics of the Educators   35

3. Challenges Are Every Day
 Prevailing Challenges Facing the Educators   53

4. If I Made a Difference for One
 Intrinsic Rewards Serving Reservation Students   78

5. Not Every Child Is the Same
 Reservation Schools in the Era of No Child Left Behind   94

6. Spread Like Wildfire
 Importance of American Indian Educators   113

7. You Have to Know the Culture
 Cultural Identity and Tribal Cultural Education   130

Appendix. Methodology, Theoretical Framework, and Research with Native Peoples   152

References 163
Index 173

Preface

In the spring and fall of 2010, I met and interviewed twenty-one American Indian educators serving Native students enrolled in reservation schools. In this book I tell the story of how the people I met defined their primary roles as educators, the prevailing challenges hindering their efforts, the most significant intrinsic rewards they perceived, and the unique pressures associated with meeting the requirements of No Child Left Behind (NCLB) for reservation schools. This book also details their perceptions and experiences on the cultural identity issues facing both students and themselves. The theme throughout the book is the hope and optimism displayed by the educators I met.

I take a narrative approach in this book. Thus, I make liberal use of excerpts from the interviews. Few messages are more powerful than the personal accounts of the educators themselves—certainly more so than my poor attempts to summarize their experiences. The book presents their quotations unaltered in grammar and syntax. My objective is to convey the humanity, dilemmas, frustrations, and hopes of American Indian educators serving reservation communities as they related those experiences to me.

Curiously, scholars have largely ignored this obviously important group of Native professionals. Likely, I would have, too, except that ideas for research can come in some seemingly random moments. The idea for this research came to me in an unexpected way.

Even in August, mornings along the Oregon coast can be downright cold. I have sometimes been accused of being a workaholic (at least my family thinks so; I'm not so sure about my department chair), so while attending my university's annual faculty retreat and warming up through my morning ritual of coffee I immersed myself in a recently published research article.

In this particular article, Erickson, Terhune, and Ruff (2008) report findings from their research on work satisfaction with teachers (both Native and non-Native) serving schools with large enrollments of American Indian students. The article outlines the conceptual validity and statistical reliability of using the *Quality of Teacher Work Life Survey* among educators of Native students. It presents important information, especially for quantitative researchers interested in measuring work satisfaction among educators. Two simple sentences in particular caught my attention, however. Erickson and her colleagues argue, "Maintaining highly qualified teachers in schools serving predominately indigenous student populations is a significant problem" (2008, p. 2). A few paragraphs later they add, "Teachers enter the teaching profession for intrinsic factors" (p. 3). I had no doubts about the veracity of either of these claims. Not only do they sound correct, but also I know they are true, intuitively and empirically. However, it also didn't take long for me to complete the circle of reasoning. If educators enter the profession for intrinsic reasons and it is difficult to maintain highly qualified teachers in American Indian communities, surely those who remain must do so largely for intrinsic reasons as well.

As the coffee began to take effect, my thoughts took me further. What specific kinds of intrinsic rewards do American Indian educators serving reservations experience? How do they define their role to the children and communities they serve? How does their self-defined role connect with the intrinsic rewards they perceive? Rewards in teaching always come with challenges. What challenges do they encounter? Is how they define their role associated with the challenges they identify as most vexing? Ultimately, do the intrinsic rewards outweigh the challenges? Little did I know at the time how eager American Indian educators were to talk to me about those very same issues I pondered over hot coffee on a cold morning along the Pacific coast.

I suspect that no one truly writes a book alone. That is certainly true in my case. Numerous individuals assisted with the research that led to the book, the review and editing of the manuscript, and the publication process. The leadership of Patrick Allen, Scot Headley, Linda Samek, and Gary Tiffin was nothing short of critical to the successful completion of this work. I cannot sufficiently express my gratitude for their support for this project. In similar regard, I am especially thankful for the support of the entire Department of Educational Foundations and Leadership at George Fox University who offered me the most important resource necessary for research and writing—time. Specially, I thank Sue Harrison, whose friendship and encouragement sustained me. I also appreciate the patient assistance of fellow qualitative researcher Justine Haigh, School of Business at George Fox University. Justine possesses the unique capacity to say just the right words to nudge my thought along. Her help was especially important during a brief but critical period on a related project. Ultimately, the insight she offered served to assist in the final stages of writing this book.

I am grateful for the constructive feedback of the Ed.D. students enrolled in my advanced qualitative research methods course in the summer of 2011. These students offered considerable reaction to the findings and implications reported in the book. Many of the rich discussions we shared found their way into the interpretation of the findings. I am also indebted to a team of Native scholars and educators who served as an advisory committee to oversee the research effort. These gifted individuals include Mark Carlton, George Fox University; Mike Cutler, Boise State University; Dawn Smith, Warm Springs Elementary School; and Rosemary White Shield, Minnesota Indian Women's Resource Center.

I appreciate the professionalism of the staff at the University of Nevada Press. They are a wonderful group to work with. Most notable is the support, encouragement, and guidance offered by Matt Becker. Thanks a lot, Matt! I am also indebted to Alison Hope for her diligent effort in editing this book. I owe a great deal to her attentive eye for detail.

Finally, I appreciate the love and support of my family through the research and writing process. Especially, thanks to Colleen, who helped me find the right voice.

American Indian Educators in Reservation Schools

Introduction

My rule in kindergarten was there is no such thing as "I can't." I'd say to the children, "Look at me! I'm just a poor, little Indian girl who walked up the creek every day, and look at my wall. I've got my degrees. If I can sit in this chair, you guys can, too."
—South Dakota elementary school principal and former kindergarten teacher

The earth meets the sky in this part of America. I had just passed through a village where but a small number of souls live in a few dilapidated dwellings in one of the most remote districts of a South Dakota reservation. Cresting a ridge a few miles outside the village, I could not see a person, a building, or even a tree. The emptiness of the landscape betrayed the notion a school should somehow be out here. The prairie, long since burnt over and brown by this early October day, presented a stark yet strangely compelling vista. It held a "lonesome beauty," an old Appalachian phrase to describe places of tragedy and legacy. Indeed, the very geography itself seemed to reflect the commingling of the heritage, the history, the heartbreak, and the hope of the people who live here.

The Northern Plains frequently hide surprises from the casual observer. At the top of yet another lonely ridge, a single sign, one of the few non-natural objects visible, pointed the way to the elementary school. I pulled the car onto to a poorly maintained narrow path of a road that led down the backside of the hill. As the road twisted its way downward, the terrain began to reveal lushness absent on the higher plains. Coming around a sharp turn at the bottom of the hill, a small bridge emerged that led across a creek lined by elm and cottonwood trees. In a pleasant gulch obscured from the prairie above, a school building sat beside the creek. Clearly constructed sometime in the first half of the twentieth century, the building appeared nearly square yet rather tall, rendering a top-heavy appearance. Later I would learn the school is about seventy-five years old. Walking up steps and through the front entrance, I observed the boys' restroom to the right with a sign over the door reading *"Wicasa."* Directly opposite on the left side of the hall a corresponding girls' restroom displayed a sign indicating *"Winyan."* A considerable number of impressive murals depicting traditional tribal life adorned the school while inspirational quotes from American Indian leaders added to the ambience. The school is located in one of the most culturally traditional districts of the reservation and most of the educators are Native persons, fluent speakers of their tribal language, and products of one of the three tiny communities served by the school. As subsequent interviews with the American Indian educators would reveal, the school not only looks but also functions consistent with tribal values and perspectives.

Admittedly, in many important respects this school is not typical of the schools I visited during the spring and fall of 2010. Nevertheless, the school and the people I met there exemplify the spirit that consistently greeted me in my sojourn commonly known as research. Despite complex, pervasive, and enduring difficulties, these educators displayed an unconquerable optimism in their contributions to the future of their people. Ultimately, the American Indian educators who participated in this research project revealed a unique and ubiquitous conviction that they could and would make a difference.

NATIVE FAITH

This book is about research with twenty-one American Indian educators serving reservations on the Northern Plains. It reports findings on a number of important issues to Native teachers and principals. Among other considerations, I was interested in learning how these American Indian educators describe the primary roles they perform, the intrinsic rewards and prevailing challenges they experience, and their thoughts on teaching in reservation schools during the era of No Child Left Behind (NCLB). In the following pages, I present the experiences and perceptions of the individuals who participated in this effort as faithfully and honestly as possible. But this book is more than a report of research findings. Ann Lieberman and Lynne Miller (1992) write, "A teacher operates out of a kind of blind faith that with enough in the way of planning, rational schemes, objectives, and learning activities some learning will take place" (p. 3). No doubt most teachers operate under this canopy of hope, yet the educators I met likely supplement the "blind faith" Lieberman and Miller refer to with another unique quality—a quality that can be termed "Native faith."

I had stopped for gas at the same convenience store on a South Dakota reservation on a couple of occasions and the woman who worked there did not recognize me as any of the locals or from one of the border towns. She was curious as to why I was there on her reservation. I told her a little about my research on American Indian educators and mentioned that I was very impressed by the devotion displayed by the people I had met. She smiled and said, "Ah yeah, they have that Native faith." I didn't think much about it at the time, but the phrase stayed with me and I found myself replaying that conversation as I drove the many miles across the high plains from reservation to reservation and from school to school. I had never heard the term before and perhaps she simply invented it for the sake of our conversation. Whatever the case, I believe she meant that against the social and personal sufferings afflicting reservations, many American Indians remain optimistic about their people and tribal traditions. This simple yet profound expression described the educators I encountered during the research investigation. Even though burdened by the seemingly overwhelming challenges they face on a daily basis, they strive on with hope, dedication, and vision. This book reports a research investigation but is really about Native faith.

Like any research activity, this research contains three fundamental elements. First, research must have a focus. Essentially, what does the researcher want to know? Second, research must have a purpose. Namely, why is it important that a researcher examine a particular topic? Third, research has an intrinsic nature. Basically, how does the researcher search for the answers to his or her questions? Taken together, the three components—focus, purpose, and nature—form the heart of what it means to conduct scholarly research. The findings and insights outlined in this book derived from these three parts. I began with a focus, a set of questions to which I sought answers. I framed the questions against an important sociocultural and historical background. The purpose of the work is straightforward enough: many American Indian reservations are distressed and educators offer hope for the future. Thus, the findings have some currency, and are important to a variety of people for a number of reasons. And finally, the work behind this book took a specific nature. I set about to systematically seek answers to my questions by following certain distinct, required procedures. Let me trace a little about the focus, purpose, and nature of the research because these features will most assuredly inform the findings reported later on.

The Focus: Dichotomy of American Indian Reservations

Many reservations are dichotomous places. They offer the best chances for language and cultural preservation (Figueira, 2006; Lomawaima & McCarty, 2006; Robertson, Jorgensen, & Garrow, 2004) but they are also sites of severe social and historical trauma (Cornell & Kalt, 2000; Villegas, 2006). American Indian teachers ply their profession against this backdrop. Educators on America's reservations face ponderous challenges. As in many rural areas, teacher shortages plague reservations (Ballou & Podgarsky, 1995; Boyer, 2006; Osterholm, Horn, & Johnson, 2006). Reservation schools tend to experience higher teacher turnover rates compared to nonreservation schools (Chavers, 2000; Miller Cleary & Peacock, 1998). This pattern persists despite the tendency for reservation schools to offer higher salaries and lower student-to-teacher ratios than nonreservation schools (Erickson et al., 2008). Moreover, a shortage of teachers of American Indian heritage compounds these challenges (Boyer, 2006). Ultimately, few problems besetting reservation education may be more serious than the related issues of a shortage of teachers on reservations and the lack of American Indian educators.

Typically, researchers have investigated these issues using quantitative approaches to examine the extrinsic rewards related to teaching in schools enrolling American Indian children (Erickson et al., 2008). While these efforts have produced important insights, they are limited in their ability to probe into complex personal and cultural phenomena (Swisher & Tippeconnic, 1999). As a result, the intricate connections between American Indian educator's intrinsic rewards, everyday challenges, and the self-defined roles they play with their students and communities remain largely unexplored.

It is intriguing that, despite the current emphasis on culturally relevant pedagogical practices, schools and educational policy still largely reflect the cultural mandates of mainstream society (Deloria & Wildcat, 2001; Forbes, 2000). Frequently, Native peoples find themselves culturally at odds with many educational practices (Cajete, 2006; Klug & Whitfield, 2003). Most notable in this regard is the near national obsession with standardized testing used to gauge student, teacher, and school performance. Standardized testing dominates the current educational climate in the United States (Beaulieu, 2008; Hess, 2008; McGuinn, 2006; Phillips, 2006; Ravitch, 2010). As a result, some suggest that the dilemma for a significant number of American Indian educators is not merely to be good teachers, but rather to be effective educators and still remain Indian (Ambler, 1999; Beynon, 2008; Lomawaima & McCarty, 2006).

Thus, the focus of this research was to explore a number of complex issues including the self-defined roles, the intrinsic rewards, and the challenges identified by American Indian educators serving reservation students and communities. Additionally, I was interested in their views on the prominence of standardized testing mandated by NCLB and the possible implications for American Indian students and reservation schools. I interviewed a small sample of American Indian teachers and principals serving children attending reservation schools with the goal of answering five fundamental questions:

1. How do the participants describe their roles as American Indian educators serving reservation students and communities?
2. What do the participants identify as their most compelling intrinsic rewards and challenges in serving reservation students and communities?
3. Is there a relationship between the roles the participants self-describe and the intrinsic rewards and challenges they identify?
4. How do the participants regard the impact of No Child Left Behind, especially the emphasis on standardized testing, on their students and schools?
5. Will the participants report they recognize the need to build the cultural identity of their students as suggested by a specific theoretical perspective known as transculturation theory?

The Purpose: American Indian Educators Serving Reservation Students

The institution of education has a dubious history for many American Indian peoples. It was extensively used as a mechanism of forced assimilation (Reyhner & Eder, 2004). Yet today some charge that educational mandates represent culturally coercive policies that are insensitive, if not deliberately destructive, to the cultural integrity of Native tribes (Forbes, 2000; Lomawaima & McCarty, 2006). The combined effects of historical abuse along with culturally maladroit educational practices have produced a climate in which some Native people still regard schools as foreign institutions designed by and for non-Natives (Lipka & Mohatt, 1998; Peshkin, 1997).

American Indian educators have committed themselves to serving their people through an institution that is not always highly regarded and, in fact, is frequently viewed with suspicion (Deyhle, 1992; Ward, 2005). Yet they realize the importance of their work. Thus, this research is important for a number of significant reasons. Despite the obvious importance of American Indian educators to reservation communities, researchers have largely ignored them. Researchers have examined American Indians enrolled in teacher preparation programs (Bergstrom, 2009) and Native and non-Native educators serving American Indian students (Erickson et al., 2008; Miller Cleary & Peacock, 1998). There has been little research specifically focusing on American Indian educators who serve reservation schools, however (Cherubini, 2008; Hill, Vaughn, & Brooks-Harrison, 1995). On a purely academic level, there is much to learn about the experiences and perceptions, and successes and failures of American Indian educators.

Certainly, the findings are important to those who train educators to serve reservation students as well as to American Indians who desire to enter the profession of education. The book outlines many of the challenges and the intrinsic rewards associated with serving as an educator in reservation schools. The challenges are significant, frequently tragic, and altogether inescapable. The rewards are powerful, often surprising, and ultimately sustaining. The experiences offered by these participants offer much to those willing to learn from them.

There are additional, just as compelling, reasons for studying this topic. The findings reported in this book are important to reservation communities—most notably tribal leaders and Native parents. Found in reservation schools are their neighbors, American Indian people, who offer their service, their gifts, and their sacrifice in order to prepare Native children for the future. They make enormously important contributions not only to individual students, but also to the reservation at large. Simply put, the voices of the participants in this study reveal how much they need and desire the support of the community, parents, and tribal leaders.

Finally, the research is important to Native educators. The general response to my invitation to participate in this research effort is revealing. A few examples of the replies I received include these:

> I would be honored to participate in an interview. I would like to thank you for allowing me to participate. I would love to do the interview because it will benefit our people in some way and I would like to build awareness of the shortage of [name of tribe] teachers. Thank you.
>
> I'm grateful for your research with Native people. This helps people like me in supporting American Indian students to succeed and go on to college—or whatever their postsecondary adventures might take them.
>
> I have looked at your website and found this interesting and would like to help in your endeavors. I live here in [name of the community] and have been raised on the [name of the reservation]. I continue to live here and plan on staying here for the duration of my life. My family is here and I like to hope that I am making a difference in all of our children's lives. Please let me know more information as you deem fit. Thanks.

About half of the educators I contacted did not wish to participate or were unable to do so. But those who did agree to an interview displayed a remarkable enthusiasm for the project. These educators had a story to tell and they wanted to tell it. The interviews generated a large amount of rich and nuanced information. I make no pretense of reporting all the findings in this book. Nevertheless, I want to relate the most significant insights produced by the interviews. By offering their voices, it is my intent that the book will authentically communicate their collective story as educators serving reservation children.

The Nature: A Research Journey

The appendix provides the technical details on the research methodology, analytical procedures, and theoretical framework behind the investigation. However, I need to outline the essential elements of the research in order to provide context for the findings reported in the ensuing chapters. Fundamentally, the objective was to learn more about the experiences and perceptions of American Indian educators who serve reservation children. Thus, I restricted the study to include only American Indian teachers and principals who were certified, working in schools located on a reservation. This parameter actually proved to be one of the most significant challenges in the investigative endeavor. Namely, there are few Native educators. Locating and contacting individuals who met the research criteria initially presented a significant problem. Nevertheless, using information provided on state educational associations and school websites along with the personal direction of tribal officials, school superintendents, and principals, I assembled a sample list of American Indian educators meeting the research specifications.

Ultimately, I conducted the research on five reservations located in Montana and South Dakota and engaged twenty-one educators in semistructured personal interviews. Eleven of the individuals were on Montana reservations and ten were on South Dakota reservations. The sample includes more women (fifteen) than men (six), and a greater number of teachers (fourteen) than principals (seven). The sample includes more participants in elementary schools (twelve) than in middle schools and high schools (nine). Additionally, the sample generally consists of veteran professionals. The average age for the sample is forty-seven years old (with a range of thirty-one years old to sixty years old). The average length of professional experience for the sample is eighteen years (with a range of three years to thirty-three years). Because I agreed not to reveal the specific reservations and to help protect the anonymity of the participants who came from reservations with only a few Native educators, I will not disaggregate information on the respondents. Rather, I will present information and findings in either aggregate form or in general terms. I generally refer to a specific participant by only his or her professional position and state location.

In the process of conducting each interview, I worked from a set of guide questions in order to address the five research questions driving the investigation. I left room to explore unexpected issues that arose during the interviews, however. Thus, the research resulted in a number of important extemporaneous questions. Moreover, the interviews also produced an incredible amount of data. The appendix offers a detailed description of the data analytical procedures. Suffice it to say here that the analysis of the data essentially involved a search for "themes." A theme represents a shared perception or experience articulated by the participants. I attempted to identify and describe important themes in some detail and dignify each with a label. In this book, I generally use an arbitrary threshold to identify themes. Usually, I present only the themes discussed by seven (one-third) or more of the participants. There was simply too much information to do otherwise.

In addition to the articulation of themes, throughout this book I identify a number of important theoretical constructs. Theoretical constructs are more abstract than specific themes. I conceive a theoretical construct as a conceptual umbrella under which are found several themes. For instance, the analysis of the data led me to conclude there are two types of educators, each defined by specific roles they perform. Thus, the type of educator is a general theoretical construct, and each of the educator's roles that work to define the kind of educator is a specific theme.

TWENTY-ONE STORIES

Twenty-one people, twenty-one stories—taken together the educators had nearly four hundred years of experience with reservation students. They held a reservoir of knowledge and wisdom. It was my honor to meet, talk, and get to know these individuals. It was also a compelling experience for all of us. It is no exaggeration to say that about half of the educators broke down and cried at some point in the interview, so powerful were their experiences and convictions. As I reflect on the nature of the interviews, I ask myself, What is the most important sentiment, experience, and perception these educators conveyed? My answer is that they hurt and yet they hope.

The educators I interviewed—all of them—serve distressed communities.

To them the difficulties besetting their communities were not abstract social problems. On a daily basis, the sufferings of the reservation enter their classrooms and are projected in the lives of their students. For these educators, reservation social problems were personal and had a young face. Throughout this research, I found professional educators who cared profoundly for their students, people, and communities. So much so, in fact, that they carried a burden likely unrecognized by many people in their respective communities. I wonder if even many tribal leaders understand the emotional encumbrances weighing on American Indian educators. Indeed, the extent of the pain and stress is hard to imagine and difficult to express. One teacher told me that in thirteen years of teaching she had lost at least one student each year to suicide. The Indian Health Service estimates that approximately one-third of the students enrolled in a middle school I visited were afflicted with a sexually transmitted disease. Many of the participants told stories of visiting former students in prison and lamented the wasted potential.

Yet the educators also were filled with hope. I was amazed by their optimism and, frankly, I found it inspirational. The knowledge that they make a difference to individual students and contribute to the future of the community sustains them. They related many tremendous success stories. They could point to achievements frequently involving students who, by any rational estimation, should not succeed.

Every one of the individuals I met recognized his or her responsibilities as community leaders. These educators straddle a chasm between hope and despair. They offer vision and direction to students, they lead by example, and they make efforts that frequently make significant contributions toward preserving tribal traditions and language. It is true these educators carried a great deal of hurt, but they also were sustained by an efficacious hope. I believe a Montana principal spoke for all the participants when, with a resolute voice, he said, "When you have been here long enough they trust you. You can help so much here. And I think that is the thing. If you got into education for the kids, this is the place. Because we do have a lot of problems within the community. . . . The kids here see we are beacons of hope for them."

LOOKING AHEAD

Chapter 1 outlines the findings on one of the key questions behind this investigation: the self-defined roles the participants articulated they perform as educators serving reservations. This chapter also introduces an important typology of two kinds of educators: affinitive educators and facilitative educators.

This typology is foundational to the study; throughout the remainder of the book I compare the two kinds of educators. Chapter 2 introduces the personal background and pathways into the profession of education among the participants. It also offers a description of their academic training, nature of their careers, and career goals. Chapter 3 outlines the prevailing challenges the participants identified as most perplexing, while chapter 4 reports important intrinsic rewards they described. Both chapters 3 and 4 compare and contrast the kinds of challenges and intrinsic rewards articulated by affinitive educators and facilitative educators. Together these chapters answer two of the fundamental research questions of this investigation. Chapter 5 presents the participants' experiences of serving reservation schools during the era of NCLB. Additionally, it delves into their perceptions on the impact of this policy on reservation schools and children. In chapter 6 I explore a number of interrelated cultural issues. This chapter identifies the participants' views on the need for American Indian educators as well as ways to increase the number of Native teachers and administrators. It also explores how some of the participants indicated that tribal cultural strengths enhance their professional effectiveness. Finally, chapter 7 uses the theory of transculturation to examine tribal identity issues and the nature of American Indian cultural education in reservation schools. It concludes by retracing the research questions and the most significant findings resulting from this investigation, along with possible theoretical and applied implications.

CHAPTER 1

Hope for a Better Tomorrow
Affinitive Educators and Facilitative Educators

> *I know I am affecting their lives in ways that they might not comprehend now and I might not comprehend now . . . [and] that I've made a little bit of a dent in their lives and in the Indians finding a better way. . . . Hopefully my legacy when I'm gone is that I gave these guys a lot of hope for a better tomorrow.*
> —Montana principal discussing his role as educator on the reservation

I had a little time between interviews and decided to look around the small community served by the elementary and high schools. The crumbling remains of a sidewalk led across a bridge spanning the creek and up the hill to where most of the village buildings lay. I carefully stepped over the broken glass scattered on the ground outside a large building that at one time had housed the tribal community college. Even though badly in need of repairs, the building now holds an assortment of tribal service offices. The few individuals gathered outside seemed to give me little notice, but I could feel their eyes following me, and occasionally I would catch a glimpse of their curious glances.

The cluttering of small, battered houses with tiny yards seemed older than they likely were, and I noticed even the lone tribal police SUV had cracked windows and dents too numerous to count. A softball field overgrown with brown weeds, partially bounded by a broken-down fence, the infield littered with shattered beer bottles, hinted of better use in former days. Clearly, no games had been played there for some time and it would take quite an effort to ready it again for its intended purpose. Only a monument honoring the reservation's veterans appeared preserved and untouched by vandals. Indeed, small, personal memorials placed by grateful, sincere hands lined its base.

Unfortunately, many people do not get past these and similar images common to many American Indian reservations. As a result, they frequently form oversimplified perceptions and explanations that in turn give birth to sympathy from some and distain from others. Yet these images reveal only part of reservation reality. Life is hard, but hope pervades. The hardships are easily found, but so is the hope, if one knows where to look. Perhaps more than anywhere else, educators display that hope in their resolute service to reservation schools.

THE GREATEST ACT OF OPTIMISM

The American Indian educators who participated in this research possessed a determined desire to serve their people. The theme of service permeated the interviews and their voices portrayed individuals of caring, concern, and commitment. Certainly, these qualities describe most teachers and principals. But I sense a unique essence in the desire to serve, among the participants of this investigation. These Native educators recognized the stakes are high; it is not a cliché to say the future of the reservations depends on their efforts. If, as educator and author Colleen Wilcox says, "Teaching is the greatest act of optimism," for the educators of this study it is also an act of hopefulness tempered with urgent realism. The stark social conditions of their respective reservations served to underscore the importance of their work. Some of the educators in this study expressed frustration, despondency, even despair. A few indicated an inclination to throw up their hands and quit the profession. Virtually all identified vexing difficulties for which they have few answers. Yet, with a heart for service, steeled by the constant reality of human tragedy, and fortified by hope for the future, they persevere.

The notion of vocation generally has two meanings. In a more mundane conception, "vocation" simply refers to an occupation, a set of skills and practices necessary to perform a job. In its original and more powerful sense, "vocation" invokes the idea of service (Hansen, 1994). People frequently associate a vocation with professions incorporating a higher calling, such as the clergy or medicine (Gustafson, 1982). Likewise, most people esteem teaching as more than merely an occupation. Teaching, too, is a vocation involving a noble purpose. As Liesveld, Miller, and Robison (2005) remind us, "More than a job, teaching is a calling" (p. 12).

David Hansen (1994) contends that vocation reaches its greatest expression when an awareness of public obligation intersects with personal fulfillment. In this regard, vocation entails two powerful dimensions. First, it includes a deep commitment to others resembling a ministerial call to higher service (Williams, Massaro, Airhart, & Zikmund, 2004). Second, a vocation works to define a person's life: it renders not only meaning and purpose, but also personal identity (Lieberman & Miller, 1992; Palmer, 2007). The American Indian educators in this study articulated a sense of vocation incorporating both of these dimensions. I found virtually all the participants, especially those from more culturally traditional backgrounds, to be profoundly spiritual people. They spoke easily and naturally about their personal spirituality and how it directs their purpose as educators. Many would likely agree with the South Dakota teacher who said of her vocation, "I hope I've made some type of impact on the kids academically, as well as socially and spiritually, because I think that spiritual correctness is about who we are, how we are connected to everything. Once the kids know that and see that, it makes them whole and makes them able to move on and go on. I see a lot of our kids who are lost. I wish I could take a lot of what I have and what I know and teach it to everybody and talk to them."

The educators also integrated service into their personal identities. Service, simply but significantly, defined these individuals. One South Dakota principal actually began our interview by saying, "I'm from here at [name of community]. I grew up here. I went to school here. I just walked right up the creek. So basically [name of the school] is who I am. I'm from a large family. I am very proud of who I am as a Native American and what I have accomplished. And I am here for the kids. That's really who I am."

A number of scholars have documented how American Indian educators commonly regard their profession as a call to service rather than a convenient occupation (Beynon, 2008; Chavers, 2000; Cherubini, Kitchen, & Trudeau, 2009; Cherubini, Niemczyk, Hodson, & McGean, 2010; Pavel, Banks, & Pavel, 2002). Using a case study, Hill and colleagues (1995) documented the profound commitment to use the position as educator to positively influence students and communities among five American Indian educators. Especially prominent in the findings is the emphasis placed on instilling pride in their students' tribal identity.

In a series of studies, Lorenzo Cherubini (Cherubini 2008; Cherubini et al., 2009; Cherubini et al., 2010) has chronicled the experiences of Canadian First Nation educators. His investigations reveal a common vision among First Nations educators to use their profession to build Native communities. Most notable among Cherubini's findings is the felt responsibility to assist in tribal cultural preservation. Nevertheless, as he admits, the "literature is virtually silent" (Cherubini, 2008, p. 44) on the nature of the specific roles Native professionals perceive they perform as educators.

In one of the few studies designed to explore the self-described roles assumed by Native educators, Friesen and Orr (1998) found that the First Nations educators in their investigation deliberately attempted to preserve tribal culture, presented themselves as a role model to students, and worked to positively influence the community. This study notwithstanding, most studies offer global accounts on how Native educators see their professional contributions to their peoples (Duquette, 2002). While such examinations are valuable, greater insight is needed to more fully appreciate the service Native teachers and principals render to reservation communities. Thus, I was particularly anxious to learn what the participants had to tell me about the roles they perform as educators. Understandably, the individuals in this study did not perceive that they engage in just one role. Rather, multiple roles characterized their service. In fact, the participants diverged in the way they described their primary responsibilities as educators. I treat these groups as a typology consisting of two types of educators. Furthermore, I distinguish between two kinds of roles the participants described.

TYPOLOGY OF EDUCATORS

The analysis of the data led me to identify two theoretical constructs that I present here as a typology of educators: affinitive educators and facilitative educators. Essentially, affinitive educators emphasize the importance of building interpersonal relationships and chiefly endeavor to be effective role models, while facilitative educators stress the practical benefits of educational achievement and primarily strive to be effective classroom teachers.

I began to recognize that the participants differed in the way they described their roles before completing all the interviews. I made numerous theoretical notes on this issue in my field notes, and thus while still in the field I began to develop an analytical framework. After all the data were collected and the interviews transcribed, I discovered overlapping themes in the way the participants discussed their roles. For instance, five themes consistently clustered in the responses of one group of educators. These themes are serving as a role model, developing personal relationships with students, providing encouragement, interacting with parents, and functioning as a family member. I consider these themes to be specific dimensions of the theoretical construct I call affinitive educators. A second set of five themes tended to cluster in the responses of other educators. These themes are performing the role of an effective educator, promoting the benefits of education, acting as an academic and personal motivator, operating as an agent of change, and acting as a caretaker of children. Consequently, I treat these latter themes as dimensions of the theoretical construct referred to as facilitative educators.

I then arranged each individual participant into the theoretical schema. Specifically, I classified each participant based on the way the themes clustered in his or her interview along with the global description of the roles he or she performed. Generally, the participants offered clear portrayals of their perceived roles, so classifying individual educators as either affinitive or facilitative proved a relative easy task.

As is the case with virtually all social science research, however, the findings disclosed complexities compounding intricacies. A close examination of the data revealed two kinds of roles identified by the participants. Some of the roles appear to cluster together and thereby define the two kinds of educators as described above. More to the point, the participants I refer to as affinitive educators tended to articulate five roles that are more or less idiosyncratic to that group, whereas the participants I call facilitative educators outlined five different roles more or less distinctive to them. I refer to these roles as definitional roles because they essentially distinguish one type of educator from another in terms of how the participants described their responsibilities (and presumably their professional identities).

In addition to definitional roles, I also found the participants shared important common ground in their professional experiences. Both groups described two significant roles they perform. In relative equal proportion, they expressed the necessity to use their profession as a means to help preserve tribal culture, and they related the need to be involved in the community. These two roles I refer to as foundational roles because they appear to undergird the efforts of virtually all the participants, regardless of the definitional roles they described. Thus, while working to preserve tribal culture or involving himself or herself in the community may not have been the first roles the participants discussed, they were two roles that virtually all the participants seemed to agree they must perform as Native educators.

Definitional Roles Delineating Affinitive Educators

Affinitive educators emphasized the similarities between themselves and their students. They regarded themselves primarily as role models and thus reported cultivating interpersonal relationships with students and the wider community. I classified twelve of the twenty-one participants as affinitive educators. While they recognized the need for Native children to receive a quality education, they nevertheless tended to focus on meeting personal or emotional needs as much as academic ones. As mentioned, the five definitional roles tended to converge, and thus I delineated affinitive educators as serving as a role model, developing personal relationships with students, providing encouragement, interacting with parents, and functioning as a family member.

Serving as a role model constitutes the most prominent theme defining affinitive educators. All twelve of the participants I classify as affinitive educators identified being a role model as a critical function they perform. These educators regarded themselves as examples of academic and personal success. Many Native students do not have successful role models to emulate, thus the educators understood how significant their example could be to students. Typical of this sentiment, a Montana principal explained the role of a principal in a Native school:

> My role right now is number one to be a role model. This is what you can achieve. You don't have to leave here. You can go for a while and come back and all sorts of things. But you can accomplish what you want to accomplish. I think that is the main focus right now: I want them to have role models that they can look up to that they can see as people in positions of authority that are doing a good job and are helping them see that education is important no matter what others may say or what may be going on.

Affinitive educators realized the power of role models to American Indian children. They regarded their own personal experiences as illustrations of potential opportunities their students might not otherwise recognize. For instance, a Montana educator said, "I think my role to Native children is to be a role model, first of all, to show kids that there's more. I mean, you can be whoever you want, whatever you want to be, whoever you want to be, and there are choices. . . . You can choose to stay here, which I did for twenty some years, and work with my people, or I can choose to go out to someplace else, which I've also chosen to do."

The influence of role models on reservation students cannot be overemphasized. Research has shown that impoverished children often lack adults who model academic and occupational achievement, and thus potentially develop limited visions of their own life prospects (Elliott et al., 2006). Reservation schools are commonly populated by non-Native staff whose examples likely do not include the same potency as the demonstrated success of American Indian educators (Ambler, 1999, 2006; Chavers, 2000). Little wonder, the professionals I spoke with emphasized the importance of serving as a role model and consciously worked to influence students through their personal examples.

Affinitive educators esteemed building personal relationships with their students as essential. They recognized that many students require and desire personal connections with their teachers, so they regarded relationship building as one of the most crucial roles they perform in their schools. The perspective of a South Dakota teacher illustrates this view:

> Everyone has all these answers and all these ways people are going to learn today when the real answer, I think, is just in making more connections with the kids. You know, giving them that personal touch, that personal attention, because that is more lasting and that's how they learn. I think we lose that personal touch. The kids as it is grow up in a world where even the parents don't have that personal connection. Their babysitters are a TV, video games. . . . The kids need that personal connection and it's very hard for them to cope.

For many of the participants, their own personal example underscores the relationships they forge with students, so serving as a role model reinforces personal relationships. A Montana educator stressed this point: "That's the reason I came back. . . . There has got to be something I can do. [Begins to talk more slowly with emphasis.] And part of that is being a positive role model. . . . And I try to be that example. . . . The biggest thing for me is to establish the positive. To establish positive relationships with kids. Some of these kids have no sense of being, I guess is what it is. They have no ties to school." A Montana educator echoed similar sentiments when she simply reflected, "In some ways I feel like I'm a good role model. Plus, I feel like in some ways I'm someone they can come to. Like someone they can trust. . . . Because, you know, I really think that, truly, relationships are the most important thing."

Affinitive educators regarded empathy as a major component of building personal relationships with students. They appreciated the obstacles facing students and used this understanding to build personal connections. A Montana educator spoke of the visceral tie she has with students: "I guess I can relate to the experiences that the children are going through. . . . I believe in all the research, in all the academics that I've learned, you know, I need to be firm, fair, and consistent. But I also have a heart to understand what these kids are coming from. And I believe in Maslow's hierarchy. I always have. If those basic needs are not being met, and we need to understand, yeah, we can't just say it, we need to truly understand and empathize with what the kids are going through."

Serving as a role model and working to build personal relationships with students represent complementary responsibilities in the minds of the educators. As their words illustrate, the affinitive educators rarely discussed building personal relationships without mentioning the importance of being a role model. Although these roles are conceptually different, the interviews also indicate just how intertwined they are in the daily affairs of affinitive educators. Indeed, both of these roles intersect with other roles educators play. Most notable is the responsibility to provide encouragement to students.

Affinitive educators saw themselves strategically positioned to offer encouragement to students. Likely this role naturally grows out of the effort to serve as a role model and build personal relationships. Clearly, affinitive educators were deeply moved by the emotional needs of their students and strove to help. They also described a variety of specific objectives they wanted to accomplish by encouraging students. Some of the educators attempted to enhance the self-confidence of their students. For instance, a South Dakota elementary teacher related, "I have always worked with my kids to give them self-esteem that they can compete anywhere they want to and be anything they want to as long as they work for it. And if they want it bad enough, then don't let anybody get them down. And I teach them how to do that, how to survive, how to look for answers. . . . You are going to have to learn all these things that are hard."

For a number of the affinitive educators, providing encouragement simply involved working to develop the self-worth of students. A South Dakota elementary principal spoke of the need to encourage small children who have experienced a great deal of trauma in their young lives: "I mean you have to have that will [to survive]. And how do you teach that in some of these students? They are already so broken coming from the things that they have to go through. And you just talk to them and make them feel important. That's why I say our kids have to know who they are and be proud of who they are. [Teachers need to] just get beyond schoolwork and come in and learn the three R's and treat them like somebody important, like they are."

For many of the affinitive educators this role required that they offer hope for the future. Toward that end, the importance of serving as a role model and building personal relationships was especially prominent in their accounts. In a powerful reflection, a Montana educator stated,

> I think the one thing that I give kids is hope for a better life. I live right there, right across the street. I'm connected, I'm part of these kids, I'm flesh and blood, and I think hopefully I give them that. When you start as a teacher on a reservation school—it was easy for me because I am from here—but I think you just sort of want to survive at first because things can be overwhelming. We have a lot of problems in our school, a lot of things our kids deal with. . . . They don't relate well to the Hollywoods of the world. . . . But what they do relate to are people from their own community who they can touch, who they can feel, who they can see, who have done things and now are back in the community doing things. Our kids, they need that, they need to see it, they need to feel it, they need those people around. I hope what I give them is this hope.

Providing hope involved small and large gestures. The participants described words offered as encouragement, efforts to personally intercede, and attendance at important functions celebrating the success of students. The participants cared for students; the emotional connection was clearly evident in how they described their role as educators. However, I do not believe the affinitive educators cared for their students any more than the facilitative educators did. Rather, I believe the former were simply more inclined to identify providing encouragement as a specific role they perform. In fact, as I will discuss later, the facilitative educators outlined a similar role they perform. That is, the facilitative educators expressed the responsibility to reassure and strengthen students in a different way than did the affinitive educators.

Affinitive educators lamented the lack of parental involvement in their schools but also understood its personal and historical context. Many parents do not highly regard schools, and recoil from past negative educational experiences. The participants believed they need to take the initiative to establish contact and maintain interaction with parents. A Montana educator assessed her school's efforts (and lack of efforts) to connect with parents:

> We do have some [teachers] that have developed that relationship piece with not only the students, but with the parents. And I think that's where we lack—a lot of our staff lack—that initiative to take it one step farther and develop that real relationship piece with the families. And it doesn't mean I'm always calling them when things are going bad. . . . A lot of parents won't answer, and say, "Oh my God, that's the school. I don't want to hear what they have to say." But, if you leave a message and say, "I just wanted to say that your child's doing really good today and it's such a pleasure to have them in class." So, I think they can certainly take advantage of that if they would take the initiative. . . . I see my role to the community as showing the people that the school system is not bad. Yes, historically, the school system has always been the bad guy, but times

have changed . . . and I think that some of the school personnel are finally catching on. Yeah, we need to reach out.

A Montana elementary teacher ended our interview by discussing the importance of trust that results from personal connections with parents. When I asked if there was anything she wanted to add, she replied, "I think you really need to get to know the families. The more you know the families, the more they trust you, the more you trust them. And be really patient. You have got to have lots of patience, lots of patience."

Scholars have long identified the reluctance for many Native parents to engage with schools (Davis, 1986; Philips, 1983). The fact that the affinitive educators addressed the need to interact with parents, therefore, does not come as a surprise. What is notable in their experiences, however, is the consistency to which these educators identified the context for the lack of parental involvement. Their voices indicate a keen awareness that American Indian parents have legitimate reasons for their suspicion of schools. Indeed, quite a number of the participants had their own negative educational experiences. One affinitive educator became a teacher because of the racism she believed her own children had encountered in school. More than a few described how they had been unfairly treated as schoolchildren. Affinitive educators felt the burden was upon educators to correct perceptions and make the initial strides toward healing past wounds. As a result, the affinitive educators projected a sensitive awareness of the need to proactively engage parents.

The scholarly literature certainly supports the intuitive desire to interact with parents displayed by the affinitive educators. In a study utilizing 234 American Indian parents and community leaders, Robinson-Zanartu and Majel-Dixon (1996) explored the complex relations between Native families and schools. These researchers found that although parents generally displayed suspicion toward schools, they nevertheless valued education and responded positively to culturally sensitive educators and educational practices. In light of these findings, there is every reason to believe the efforts of educators to interact with parents in culturally appropriate ways will reap positive results.

Affinitive educators also related that they sometimes must function as a family member to their students. This role, in large part, results from the social problems found on the reservations. While describing this role, they frequently noted the extent of poverty or family dysfunction in their students' lives. Moreover, the responsibility to function as a family member has a critical cultural element. Tribal members are frequently regarded as part of an extended family, and must care for one another. A Montana teacher described what this role means in her teaching experience:

> Well, sometimes it's mother. [Laughs.] Most of the time it is mother. [Laughs some more.] Mother, friend, mentor, of course teacher. And as a mother you are all these things anyway. You look in there [points to a closet in the classroom]. I have Gatorade, I have food, because sometimes they are hungry. I have a shelf in there where I keep breakfast bars and things like that. "Did you eat this morning?" We do have free lunch and free breakfast here but sometimes they don't get here until 8:30 and it [the cafeteria] is closed by then. They have to be in class but if you are hungry? They know to come here and get something. And I'm not the only one that does that.

A South Dakota elementary teacher spoke of how playing the role of family member to her students entails the responsibility to teach tribal values. This particular individual was culturally oriented and served in a traditional community on the reservation. Her approach to the education of young children reflects the expectations of her community:

> The first year I was here I had my sister's daughter in here. And she said, "You're my auntie!" And I said, "Yes I am." So another little girl said, "If she is your auntie, you're my auntie too!" . . . So in the kids' eyes they all call me grandma, they'll call me mom, they'll call me auntie. So I see myself in all those roles. At the same time, I see myself teaching the social skills of the [name of tribe]. They wanted to kill one of those ugly worms, a centipede, the other day. And I said, "No. They have a right to live too. That is their right. You have a right to live. They aren't bothering you." I told them, "I was always taught that everything has a right to live." Or when we go pick sage, I tell them, "You always offer a prayer. Don't just take it. Some of you pull these up by the root. Don't do that because they are not going to grow back the next year. You have to break them off, say a prayer, and make an offering. . . . It's whatever you have in your heart. You can even give a prayer but you are giving something back for taking that life." And then we talked about life on the playground.

As mentioned above, the responsibility to function as a family member has a powerful cultural dimension easily missed by non-Native people. Native peoples generally value and frequently operate as extended family networks (HeavyRunner & DeCelles, 2002; Mainor, 2001). By its very definition, the extended family includes many individuals who perform important family functions. For Northern Plains Indians, the extended family is not necessarily restricted to individuals sharing a blood relationship. For instance, the

Lakota concept of *tiyospaye* is a primary social unit consisting of a circle of all relatives via blood, marriage, or adoption. In practical terms, it includes virtually all members of a community. Thus, the extended family essentially involves community-based kinship. When a non-Native teacher relates she acts "like a mother" to her students, she generally means she plays a symbolic role involving mother-like functions of nurturing and caring. However, this is not the case for most of the educators who participated in this research. For these individuals, the claim to function as family member carries considerable cultural meaning. This role includes significant communal expectations and responsibilities beyond a symbolic metaphor. These participants taught tribal values and strove to ensure that children did not go hungry. They performed these actions not only because they were compassionate people (which they were), but also because they understood they must perform traditional responsibilities that rest on the shoulders of tribal leaders.

Definitional Roles Delineating Facilitative Educators

Facilitative educators include those participants who emphasized the instrumental benefits of academic success. They regarded being a proficient educator as a basic definitional role, and frequently spoke of the need to equip their students with the skills necessary for academic achievement. I treated nine of the twenty-one participants as facilitative educators. My analysis revealed five generally intersecting definitional roles that serve to delineate facilitative educators, including performing the role of effective educator, promoting the benefits of education, serving as an academic and personal motivator, operating as an agent of change, and acting as a caretaker of students.

Facilitative educators regarded their fundamental obligation to be a competent educator. Among the nine participants treated as facilitative educators, all said their primary role was to be an effective educator. They considered educational success essential for their students' future. Although these individuals recognized other important roles, they overwhelmingly emphasized the critical need to serve as efficient educators who facilitate educational achievement. A typical sentiment came from a Montana elementary teacher who explained,

> My first role is an educator. I am a disciplinarian, a motivator. Sometimes I am like a friend. It depends on the kid, it depends on the day. But it's a combination of a lot of things. A lot of roles. Most important being that they are here to learn and I have things to teach them. And from 8:15 to 3:15 they have to learn as much as possible because we

don't have a lot of time. So getting them to see the bigger picture and look down the road, have some ambition, and develop some goals and dreams [is important].

Such descriptions typified the facilitative educators. Much like the Montana educator quoted above, a South Dakota principal stated, "I think my main goal or role is that I want the best education possible for the students in my building. I really believe that education is important and if I can somehow make that connect with the students that education is your key to success in life, I think I have done my job. That is probably the biggest goal that I have in this school."

A South Dakota high school teacher spoke of the need for flexibility as an educator. The general tone of the interview underscores the facilitative nature of her efforts. She, like other facilitative educators, emphasized the need to provide effective, structured instruction for students:

> When it comes to teaching, there is kind of a dual role for me compared to the kids that are presently in my class and the kids that I previously have had who are no longer in my class. I'm pretty stringent and I'm all about procedures and structure with my kids because I know they don't always have it. And my kids just flourish when there is structure and they know the expectations, they know what is going to happen. They just do very well in that. So I am a lot more strict and the human connections come later. Because right now I want them to see me as their teacher.

Clearly the necessity to perform as a competent educator defined facilitative educators more than any other role they described. However, while the facilitative educators stressed the importance of professional effectiveness, the well-being of children was never far from their thoughts. These individuals did not strike me as mechanical, inflexible teachers and principals who were interested only in classroom instruction and management but who are unmindful of the human needs of their students. Indeed, what I saw were educators who care deeply and profoundly for Native children. Like the affinitive educators, roughly half of the facilitative educators broke down in tears at some point during the interview. Far from being emotionally distant educators, I encountered individuals who truly believe their best contribution to American Indian children is to offer the highest professional competence they possibly can. Because they cared, they worked hard to be competent.

Facilitative educators frequently discussed the options educational achievement can provide for both students and the reservation. Therefore, facilitative educators described their role to actively promote the benefits of education. A Montana teacher exemplifies this disposition:

> Honestly I think there's, in our community, a reverse racism mentality where education, doing good in school, is for whites. There's an attitude like that, I believe, and it kind of hinders kids. That education is not important. As an Indian educator, I have to combat that mentality and stress to these kids that education is important. And we talk about the problems in our community and we're trying to get these kids to see that if they are educated they can do things about the problems in our community. And that's where I try to push my kids.

A South Dakota educator addressed her responsibility to counter the underutilization of educational resources:

> While we have the resources here for everyone to be educated, for everybody to have an education, we don't use it. What can we do as a people to get that out there that if they had an education they would be so much better off? Their education is something they would have for life that nobody can take away from them. So the only thing I can do as a [name of tribe] educated female is to tell everybody and encourage them. Set goals for yourself, number one. You have to have goals. You want to be happy in life, set some goals. They don't have to be big ones, start with little tiny ones. Number two, take advantage of what we have here. We have a university right at our grasp.

A Montana principal spoke of the need to overcome generational barriers in order to promote the benefits of education. He recognized that his tribe's negative history with education impacts his role as an educator: "Some of the parents and grandparents . . . have that perception, you know, their own recollections of what their school history was like. And that's kind of hard to get over because one of the things they say is, 'Well when I was going to school. . . .' And I show them our mission statements and say, 'This is what we are,' and you are welcome to come in. . . . So part of my role, too, is overcoming those perceptions of what the school is."

In many respects, the role to promote the benefits of education for facilitative educators is similar to the responsibility to interact with parents expressed by the affinitive educators. Both types of educators recognized barriers resulting from past perceptions and experiences. Moreover, facilitative and affinitive educators realized the need to counter resistance to education on the reservation. Nevertheless, the interviews indicated they approach this task in different ways. Affinitive educators chose to engage parents. To them personal interaction was the most feasible strategy to overcome negative perceptions of schools. Facilitative educators, on the other hand, described efforts to present education and schools as inviting, promising, and consistent with tribal values when opportunities afforded themselves. Their descriptions appear to be less proactive than those suggested by the affinitive educators, but not necessarily less important. In the end, facilitative educators and affinitive educators were essentially working toward the same goal. They wanted the reservation to understand that the school was not alien to the community, but rather was part of it.

Facilitative educators held high expectations for their students. As a result, many described working hard to motivate students to achieve in school. Others discussed their attempts to inspire students in personal matters beyond academics. Whether in the classroom or outside of school, facilitative educators related that they frequently act as academic and personal motivators. A South Dakota high school teacher described this particular role in rather colorful terms:

> Basically what I am is a kick in the pants. A lot of my students have attendance problems. A lot of my students, they don't value their education and they're not successful in a classroom. . . . But I'm real upfront with my kids: "If you need to do this, then it's up to you to do this. I will be here to help you but I'm not going to hold your hand." . . . Just to give them the support that I had growing up and graduating from this school. . . . So many of my kids don't have that. And if you noticed, there is a little sign on my door that says, "I care. Stop in and visit." I will have kids standing in front of my door. From the time I walk into this building they are waiting for me. [Begins to cry.]

Indeed, she was not exaggerating. The day I met with this educator, students were lined up outside her room to meet with her.

A Montana high school teacher related how she motivates students. Moreover, she believed that she can effectively inspire students specifically because she is an American Indian educator from the reservation:

> As an educator I think that my students already have accepted me. I am from here, I'm a tribal member. . . . So it's different how they perceive me from maybe another teacher. That's what I see as the difference. They know that's where I'm from so that doesn't change for them. So I can do the other part [motivation] for them. I can say this is what you are going to need in order to succeed, this is why I am pushing you. I try to push them all because I just realize that education is going to be their key to success. . . . And I don't so much worry about offending them culturally or whatever because I try to push them.

Once again I found a close connection between the roles described by affinitive educators and those described by facilitative educators. When affinitive educators talked about encouraging students, they frequently described helping with self-esteem issues. Facilitative educators, on the other hand, were more likely to relate attempting to motivate students on either academic or personal matters. It took a lot of analysis and reflection on the data, but I eventually concluded that the participants were discussing two different concepts. The descriptions provided by the affinitive educators contained a nurturing essence. They deliberately attempted to offer hope and to lift the spirits of children. Facilitative educators, too, desired to encourage their students and the interviews documented just how emotional those efforts could be for them. Nevertheless, facilitative educators largely took an approach different from that typical of affinitive educators. Their descriptions portrayed attempts to intellectually move students. As a result, they were more likely to appeal to students' rational thinking. The efforts among the affinitive educators had a visceral quality. The efforts among the facilitative educators had a cerebral quality.

Similar to the role to promote the benefits of education, a number of facilitative educators indicated they see themselves as agents of change on the reservation. Generally, they described this role in more abstract terms than their responsibility to promote the benefits of education, although I suspect a close relationship between the two roles. A Montana teacher reflected on serving as a change agent. Significantly, he framed social change as a return to a reliance on traditional tribal values:

> I kind of see myself as an agent of change and the people who have an opportunity to change it are our generation and these kids. Because a lot of things need to change around here. A lot of negative characteristics that are not traditional. There's a lot of self-centered, selfish behaviors out there and traditionally you are supposed to see yourself as part of the whole, part of the larger group. Sometimes that perspective is kind of forgotten, it seems like. People are just looking out for themselves or just looking out for their own family. But there are people who still understand you got to look out for everybody, you got to look out for the tribe. If you can take care of these kids and give them a good head start and a good foundation, then they will take care of the next generation. So my role is kind of like a role that a lot of people played before. I preserve what has been taught to me and pass on as much as I can.

A South Dakota principal discussed his school's part, and by inference his own role, in affecting social change on his reservation: "My goal is for this school to be a model of change and we don't have one of those on the reservation." Likewise, a Montana principal outlined his vision for his school. His remarks reveal the perceived need for educators to function as change agents:

> There is going to have to be a switch in the community system, I would say, with the tribal boards, with the community itself, by saying that education is important. Just because we are on the rez doesn't mean things have to be a certain way. I guess one of my visions is . . . that the reservation is ours and we can make it whatever we want it to be. Why do we want it this way? . . . I want to defeat that, "Well this is the rez, this is way it is. We drop out when we're fifteen, we drink and we smoke, and we do these things because that's the way it is. That's the way everybody lives." Well, we need to change that portion of it. That's the main focus for me.

Facilitative educators recognized the urgency to combat the perplexing social problems found on their reservations. In their view, American Indian educators represent one of the few serious contenders as models of social change for reservation communities. Nevertheless, they displayed a great deal of frustration around this role. Facilitative educators frequently pointed to a lack of political leadership and a general disregard for education as serious obstacles to affect social change. Consequently, they also understood that the benefits produced through acting as an agent of change will likely take years to realize.

The prevalence of domestic violence is a sad reality on the reservations I visited. The participants frequently discussed the consequences of this social problem. Many of the educators, both affinitive and facilitative, addressed the necessity to provide security for their students. However, the facilitative educators were more likely to identify the caretaker role for children as a specific function they perform. Some, such as a Montana principal, spoke of this responsibility simply and directly: "My role, even as principal, is to help children be successful in school and make sure they are safe." Others, such as a South Dakota teacher, offered poignant reflections on this role: "I see the kids that come from the poorest of homes that have domestic violence in their homes. You know, once they walk in that door, they will tell us their problems. What happened that night. And we will hug them and let them know that they don't have to worry while they are at school. They just become different kids. They are just learning. I want them to feel safe and secure while they are here and that I can be trusted. That I am here for them. Because I am."

Similar to affinitive educators who discussed the need to act as a family member for students, facilitative educators also outlined their responsibility to care for students. The roles of acting as a family member and caring for the students are so close that I needed to deeply analyze the data in order to understand the nuanced difference between them. The affinitive educators generally discussed their responsibilities for the holistic welfare of students. This included not only ensuring the physical well-being of children, but also ensuring that their innate needs were met. The facilitative educators tended to describe a more narrow focus in caring for students. These participants were specifically concerned with the safety of children. They saw their role as keeping negative or dangerous elements away from students while they were in their care.

I also believe facilitative educators were inclined to mention the responsibility to care for students for much the same reason as the affinitive educators were prone to identify functioning as a family member as one of their roles. The participants operated within a cultural milieu in which the care of children is expected of tribal community leaders. The affinitive educators, as will be discussed in the next chapter, were more likely to come from culturally traditional backgrounds and, thus, more inclined to frame this role using traditional descriptions—they were a family member to students. The facilitative educators, less likely to come from tribally traditional backgrounds, were nevertheless heavily influenced by the cultural expectations of their community, yet were more inclined to concentrate on a specific dimension of caring for children—their physical safety. After all, this is what a competent educator is supposed to do.

A Montana elementary teacher summed up the thoughts of many of the participants when he declared, "Traditionally we're all supposed to take care of each other, to look out for one another, and my role in the community is to look out for these kids. Take care of them while they are here with me." Ultimately, the cultural expectation to care for children was shaped by the personal background and the professional identity of each participant. These educators, both affinitive and facilitative, were performing similar roles, but they expressed the roles in different ways.

Reflection on the Definitional Roles and Types of Educators

In their examination of teaching as a vocation, Lieberman and Miller (1992) observe that teachers engage in two critically important "missions." Teachers need to personally connect with students, while simultaneously conveying necessary academic knowledge and skills. They suggest these efforts are somewhat contradictory; the challenge for each teacher is to strike the appropriate balance between them. Educators achieve that balance only through concerted effort; once established, that balance forms the very identity of the teacher as a professional. As Lieberman and Miller (1992) explain, "The teachers, then, have two missions: one universal and cognitive, and the other particular and affective. The cognitive mission demands a repertoire of skills in moving a group and making sure that knowledge builds, extends, and is learned. The affective mission requires that teachers somehow make friends with their students, motivate them, arouse their interest, and engage them on a personal level" (p. 2). What Lieberman and Miller refer to as the affective mission is similar to my notion of affinitive educators. These individuals valued the personal relationships they forged with their students and it forms the core of their identity as educators. Conversely, what Lieberman and Miller label the cognitive mission is comparable to my conception of facilitative educators. Much like the conceptualization provided by Lieberman and Miller, facilitative educators strove to develop the intellectual and academic capabilities of their students.

Additionally, Lieberman and Miller contend elementary teachers and secondary teachers experience their profession in fundamentally different ways. Specifically, elementary teachers focus more on the affective mission of their vocation, whereas secondary teachers concentrate on the cognitive mission. In other words, the type of educational setting helps shape which type of mission will take precedence in a teacher's effort. Or, as Lieberman and Miller (1992) explain, "It is conventional wisdom that elementary teachers are child-focused and secondary teachers are subject matter focused" (p. 43).

Based on Lieberman and Miller's contention, one might suspect that the elementary educators in this study would be more inclined to describe the roles of affinitive educators and the secondary educators more likely to describe roles associated with facilitative educators, but I did not find this to be the case. Elementary and secondary educators described their roles in remarkably similar ways. I considered seven of the twelve elementary educators and five of the nine secondary educators as affinitive educators. Conversely, I treated five of the twelve elementary educators and four of the nine secondary educators as facilitative educators.

A similar argument might be made regarding the type of position an individual holds. Administrators, given the nature of their position, might be more inclined to assume facilitative characteristics over affinitive ones, but I did not find a difference in whether an individual serves as a teacher or an administrator. The seven administrators were equally split, with four considered affinitive educators and three treated as facilitative educators. This is also the case for the fourteen teachers in the sample: I treated eight as affinitive educators and six as facilitative educators.

Lieberman and Miller (1992) also suggest a gender-related difference in the school cultures found in elementary and secondary buildings. Namely, as they put it, "The secondary school faculty culture is primarily a male culture; this is in marked contrast to predominately female environment of most elementary schools" (p. 49). Based on this observation, it would be logical to assume that female educators are more likely to adopt the roles valued by affinitive educators while male educators are more apt to appropriate roles associated with facilitative educators. However, at best there is only weak evidence of this pattern and only among the female participants. The sample included fifteen women and six men. Of the fifteen women, I treated nine, nearly two-thirds, as affinitive educators and six as facilitative educators. Conversely, I considered three of the six men as affinitive educators and three as facilitative educators.

I am inclined to believe that the type of school setting, professional position, or gender has little to do with whether an individual assumes an affinitive or facilitative disposition. Rather, I believe the type of roles these educators emphasized reflects their cultural backgrounds, their pathway into the profession, and the nature of their professional training. I will offer greater consideration of these topics in the next chapter.

Foundational Roles

The participants also articulated sharing important roles. Both affinitive and facilitative educators frequently discussed helping to preserve tribal culture and being involved in the community as critical roles they perform as Native teachers and principals. I conceptualize these two roles as foundational largely because the analysis of the data suggests they support the definitional roles that delineate the two types of educators.

The sentiment that Native educators must assist in enhancing tribal language, culture, and values permeated the interviews. Both affinitive and facilitative educators agreed this is an important role they must perform. Indeed, the interviews indicated this role is foundational in every sense of the word. So important is this issue that I will address it in more detail in chapter 7.

A Montana educator, a facilitative educator, related that reservation schools need to integrate and infuse tribal values. In his view, the cultural anchoring provided by tribal values and worldview will lead to improved prospects for students as well as for the reservation. Thus, educators must recognize opportunities to preserve and teach the values of their tribe: "I think what needs to happen is there needs to be a preservation of traditional values; those need to be brought back into the school system. Those kids need to relearn what has been lost. From there they will start to see, okay, everyone needs to take care of each other. We're part of a larger group and positive things, I believe, will start to happen."

A South Dakota educator, an affinitive educator, argued that because the community and families are not teaching children tribal culture and language, schools must assume this responsibility. Specifically referring to the tribal language of her reservation, she stated that schools must be responsible "because the parents don't [teach the language]. The community doesn't. It's not like they are teaching the language, I wish they would, the community people. But it's on our shoulders now. So I do it throughout the day. I teach the language."

While generally scholars have not widely nor systematically investigated the roles performed by American Indian educators, nonetheless the obligation to strengthen one's tribal culture is a prevailing theme in the literature. For instance, in her study with fourteen First Nation teachers serving indigenous communities, Duquette (2002) found that a major motivation to become an educator was to assist in the survival of traditional tribal culture. Begaye (2007) sought to "uncover the concerns raised by Native teachers about the direction Native communities are headed regarding the status of language and culture" (p. 36). He found that the American Indian teachers in his study emphatically stressed the need to assist in tribal cultural preservation. Indeed, they regarded as one of their fundamental roles sustaining the culture. As Begaye relates, "Respondents stated that preserving, sustaining, and perpetuating language and culture in schools is critical" (Begaye, 2007, p. 43).

Consistent with previous findings, the participants, too, regarded the preservation of tribal culture as a crucial responsibility. The conclusion is clear. Generally, Native educators serving reservation communities embrace the responsibility of assisting in the preservation of tribal culture. However, one must wonder how frequently this role is taken into consideration in conventional teacher training programs or, for that matter, during in-service training. An enormous opportunity exists to employ educators in efforts to preserve tribal history, language, and traditions.

Additionally, both affinitive and facilitative educators identified community involvement as an important role they perform. Similar to the need to preserve tribal culture, I could not determine a discernible pattern in the participants' responses on this particular role. The affinitive educators and facilitative educators in roughly equal proportion mentioned involvement in the community as important; the context of the interviews indicate both groups rendered it equivalent significance. Thus, I consider this role as foundational to the mission of the educators in this study.

The participants offered a number of reasons for the importance of community involvement. Most notably, they regarded it as an essential part of the communal responsibilities expected of reservation leaders. Furthermore, it provides an opportunity for students to see them participating in the larger community outside the classroom. Thus, being active in the community reinforces the messages they attempted to convey to students in school. As a Montana teacher, a facilitative educator, explained,

> They see me as a teacher. But because I was born and raised here they also see me as a community member. I like to get involved in a number of things outside of the school. I like to go up to the jail and visit people. And I try to just get involved in events that are not even school related. And I do that number one because I care about the community and care about our people. And the kids see me at these events and they will go, "Oh [participant's name], I saw you at the powwow!" And I will go, "Yeah, I was there, I saw you dancing." Or, "I saw you at the hospital." So the kids make a connection with me outside of just teaching.

Likewise a Montana teacher, an affinitive educator, discussed her civic activities (which were quite numerous) and how she tries to impact children beyond the school grounds. Her comments demonstrate the importance this educator placed on the need to be a positive role model to her students, "I think it is good [being involved in the community]. Because, like I said, they [students] watch you, they know you, and if you mess up they will let you know. But I also don't cut them down if they are ever in JDC [Juvenile Detention Center]. I also tutor over at JDC twice a week so I know who is in there. It's not just my little kids here. I know all the kids. I go over there and I do that."

Lieberman and Miller (1999) state teachers commonly are caught in a tension between the requirements of the social institution of education and the expectations of the community. This contention derives from the unfortunate overextension of educators in contemporary society (Epstein, 2001). For well over a century, teachers have been increasingly expected not only to provide for the academic needs of students, but also to serve as social service agents. Lieberman and Miller contend,

> [T]here is the tension between the school and the larger community. Do schools operate as separate institutions dedicated exclusively to academics and matters of the intellect, or do they respond to the needs and values of the communities that surround them? Do schools complement families, or do they supplant them? These are contemporary questions, but they are not new. Since the late 19th century, when schools took on the task of socializing—as well as educating—large immigrant populations, there has been disagreement about where schools stand as part of the larger social order. What should the relationship be between parents and teachers, between school and home? Are schools social service agencies as well as educational institutions? Where are lines drawn? Where are boundaries crossed in the interest of children? (Lieberman & Miller, 1999, pp. 8–9)

The participants in this study recognized the larger community will not always support and value their mission as educators. In that sense, they experienced the tension between the school and the community identified by Lieberman and Miller. However, most of the participants, I believe, regarded their role to be both an educator of children and responsible community member responding to the needs of their people. These educators had largely resolved any ambiguity in their responsibilities to their community. They are both teacher and social service agent. They may have felt overwhelmed by the demands imposed by both sides of these responsibilities, but generally they accepted them. This acknowledgement of their social responsibilities is evidenced by their display of sustained involvement in the community. It did not matter which set of roles a person happened to emphasize, affinitive or facilitative—the individuals I met understood and accepted the necessity to assist in meeting the needs of their people by acting as engaged community members.

CONCLUSION

Carmelita Lamb (2010) has reported on the efforts to train future reservation teachers at Turtle Mountain Community College (TMCC) in Belcourt, North Dakota. What is particularly relevant to this study is how she describes the objective of the teacher preparation program there: "Here at Turtle Mountain Community College . . . we have a passion for the most important item on the education wish list: an exemplary teacher, someone who is knowledgeable, caring, and willing to make each student feel important and integral to the learning process each and every day of the school year. A model teacher values the cultural heritage of all Indian people and draws upon Native traditions and teachings to enrich and contextualize lessons" (Lamb, 2010, p. 40).

While Lamb does not use the terms "affinitive educator" and "facilitative educator," it is clear the design of the teacher preparation program at TMCC is to deliberately merge the attributes central to each type of educator and instill these traits into their future teachers. The individuals I interviewed in all likelihood have the characteristics of both affinitive and facilitative educators. With that said, I also believe they have a tendency to lean toward a certain predilection. As a result, by asking the participants to describe their roles, the interviews documented their inclination toward either an affinitive or a facilitative disposition. My intent in offering this typology of educators is not to suggest one is superior to the other: it is merely to propose an analytical framework. The fact is that reservations greatly need educators possessing both affinitive and facilitative characteristics. Indeed, given the insidious and complex challenges confronting the participants, it is impossible to conceive one type of educator alone would be sufficient to meet the needs of American Indian children and communities. Additionally, like effective educators everywhere, the participants necessarily assume a number of interpersonal styles and roles. In other words, sometimes they likely emphasized the roles associated with facilitative educators, and other times the roles typical of affinitive educators. The point is that the educators I met have complex roles to perform. Moreover, they have complex roles because they have a difficult job with tremendous demands. By necessity, they must play many different roles to a host of people and circumstances.

A critical question originally driving the research was, How do American Indian professionals regard their role as educators? The analysis of the interviews revealed the complexity underneath what would otherwise appear to be a straightforward query. The participants performed multiple roles that involve complex responsibilities. Careful consideration of the data led me to conclude that educators in this study diverge in how they described their professional roles, so I created the typology consisting of two theoretical constructs: affinitive educators and facilitative educators. The next chapter will explore more closely the personal and professional backgrounds of the educators. This examination helps reveal why the participants separated into two groups.

CHAPTER 2

Every Reason to Succeed
Characteristics of the Educators

> *I feel Indian people can have a larger impact on the reservation, especially if you are from the reservation. So I always figured that some way or another I would come back and do something. So that was kind of my goal to come back and offer whatever I had. . . . I tell kids all the time that I had every reason to fail. Absolutely every reason to fail. But I had every reason to succeed, too.*
>
> —Montana educator discussing his personal background

Too late for lunch and too early for dinner, few people congregated in the restaurant at this time of day. My next participant, like a number of others, had selected a restaurant for the interview. Initially, I was a bit concerned about the quality of the voice recordings, given the background noise common to diners. However, I was more worried about whether the participants would feel free to openly discuss their thoughts in such public places. I discovered I had little to be concerned about on either account.

The establishment was part Western saloon and part eatery, located "downtown" in the community that served as the reservation's agency headquarters. The few patrons, all Native people, displayed quite a range of preferences in attire. A couple of men wore cowboy hats and boots, while one had on baggy sweatpants and a hoodie. Another young man sported a T-shirt with cut-off sleeves and a logo of a band I did not recognize. (My kids would not have been surprised at my lack of knowledge on pop culture.) A woman I took to be the owner greeted me with a big smile and asked, "Are you waiting for [the participant's name]?" A little surprised, I said, "Yeah, I sure am." She smiled again. "Sit anywhere you want. Take your time and visit as long as you like. If you want coffee, we'll keep it coming to you!"

The participant arrived a little late to our appointment but wasted no time relating her life story and the rich experiences she had gained as an educator on her home reservation. A relatively new teacher, her career had already been very eventful. In a short period, she had experienced wonderful successes and profound tragedies. A rash of student suicides plagued the school and its community. The people of the reservation, especially this young educator, were at odds to understand the reasons why. She told me about the students she had lost. With loving detail, she described each student's personality and aspirations, and offered vignettes of each one's life. With every telling, she cried anew over the heartbreak of losing a student she truly loved. The interview was a powerful experience.

THE DEMANDS OF SERVICE

During the course of this investigation, a number of educators related the pain of losing students to suicide, to auto accidents, even to murder. Given the enormous demands placed upon them, I became more and more curious about how the people I met came to be educators and why they have such an intense desire to serve.

In this chapter, I outline the general characteristics of the educators and the paths that led them into the vocation of education. I examine the personal backgrounds of the participants, with particular focus on their early cultural socialization experiences and self-described cultural orientation as adults. I also consider the general character of their academic training, nature of their careers, and professional goals. Throughout this treatment, I compare affinitive educators with facilitative educators in order to understand how their personal and professional backgrounds might have influenced how they described their roles. The analysis of the data led me to the conclusion that the cultural background of the participants significantly influences how they defined their responsibilities as educators. Nevertheless, in many respects homogeneity characterized the educators. They shared a number of important personal and cultural experiences. Generally, the participants reported deep connections to reservations. All of them lived on and frequently raised their own children on the reservation. Perhaps the most noticeable variation among them involves their early socialization and subsequent orientation toward American Indian cultural traditions and language. Some educators clearly articulated a culturally traditional point of reference while others, just as evidently, reported a mainstream cultural orientation. Virtually all participants indicated respect and admiration for the history and traditions of their peoples, however.

Personal Background and Cultural Orientation

The typical respondent was a rural person, teaching on the reservation of his or her rearing and tribal membership, and a first-generation college graduate. Although this statement is most assuredly a generalization, it suggests common personal background characteristics shared among most of the educators.

Not surprisingly, the participants overwhelmingly came from reservations. Merely three of the twenty-one educators had spent most of their early childhood and formative years off a reservation and only as adults came to live for a sustained period on a reservation. The early childhood and formative years for two other individuals were about equally split between on and off a reservation. Although a number of the respondents had lived in large cities, typically as children, no more than two described having resided for any substantial period in a major metropolitan area. Five grew up on a different reservation from the one in which they resided at the time of the interview, thus most of the educators served on the reservation of their tribal membership and place of rearing. In fact, one-third of the participants taught or worked as an administrator in the very school they once attended in their youth. Naturally enough, this fact seems to have provided an added sense of investment for these individuals. A South Dakota elementary teacher explained her motivation for becoming an educator. The fact that she came from the reservation and had grown up with a culturally traditional orientation helped to legitimize her role as a teacher to young Native children. Moreover, she also demonstrated her frustration, both as a parent and later as a teacher, with what she considered the demeaning teaching practices of non-Native educators:

> I grew up predominantly on the reservation. . . . I've been a rez brat all my life, the majority of my life. . . . I had seen a lot of things happening when I was taking my children to school. I would see the difference in how they would treat the children [Native and non-Native]. . . . That really bothered me. . . . I wanted to be in the classroom. I did all the watchdog statistics on how our Indian kids did really low. . . . I couldn't understand why the majority of our kids were doing that. . . . So I went into teaching more or less to keep our kids interested in school.

The majority of the educators were first-generation college graduates. Fifteen of the twenty-one related their parents had either not attended or graduated from college. However, I found a notable difference between affinitive educators and facilitative educators. Almost all of the affinitive educators were first-generation college graduates (eleven out of twelve) compared to just under half of the facilitative educators (four out of nine). The participants recognized that, more often than not, many of their students will also be first-generation college students, and so personally related to the educational challenges and opportunities facing students. Consequently, a number of the educators saw themselves as exemplifying the prospects offered by educational success. For instance, a Montana middle school principal responded to an inquiry on whether he was a first-generation college graduate:

> Sure was. I think one of my proudest moments is that I went to school . . . and in four years I was back teaching. . . . I think a lot of kids, you know, you just give them some hope, some hope to survive, especially off the reservation. . . . So one of my big motivations was to not only get a degree, but to come and let people know that you can go through a lot of things in your life. I mean, you can live the rez life and you can be down and out and still persevere and do things with your life that are really difficult. Reservations have this aura of destruction and people getting out is something pretty rare.

Regarding his ability to relate as a first-generation college student, another Montana principal who also served as the school's softball coach reflected, "It helps me talk to some of the kids I coach and do some things here. I can help them try and bridge the gap that's there. It's going to be difficult. There's going to be this shock that's going to come to you. But once you get past that shock you can make it anywhere. If you can make it here you can make it anywhere."

The participants described their cultural orientation in a variety of ways. Most notably, they differed in how they portrayed their childhood and adolescence socialization experiences and in the manner they depicted their posture toward tribal culture after achieving adulthood. Seven described their childhood rearing as oriented toward the mainstream cultural society. Conversely, six identified their early years as oriented toward tribal cultural traditions with frequent participation in traditional ceremonies and use of a tribal language in the home. Indeed, all six of these individuals reported either fluency or proficiency in their tribal language. The remaining eight educators described early socialization somewhere between the mainstream and tribal cultural traditions.

Again, a revealing divergent pattern exists between affinitive and facilitative educators. While six of the twelve affinitive educators described culturally traditional early socialization experiences, none of the facilitative educators reported similar childhoods. All of the facilitative educators indicated early socialization experiences oriented toward the cultural mainstream or somewhere in between the mainstream and American Indian cultural traditions.

Whatever the nature of their early cultural socialization, virtually all the educators reflected with respect and admiration on the cultural heritage of their people. In fact, even those describing themselves as immersed in the cultural mainstream reported wanting to learn more about their culture and language. Indeed, many of the interviews suggested that the longer an educator served on the reservation, the greater his or her inclination to learn more about traditional tribal culture. Typical is the attitude of a Montana educator who described her early socialization:

> I was more assimilated, definitely assimilated. Not until, I would say, in recent years. . . . And I really attribute that to my grandparents, my mother's mom and dad, my maternal grandparents. They're the ones that taught me some about the culture. They didn't teach me a whole lot, but they introduced me to powwows and dancing, and so I had that love. . . . I really feel like it's more bicultural and I feel that I'm bicultural now at this stage in my life. Definitely I really knew very little about my culture, my heritage, until I got older. There's still a lot I do not know and I learn more every day.

Similarly, a Montana teacher mused,

> As I've got older I've taken my own interest. I grew up here. My family didn't participate in ceremonies. I went to a few sweats with my dad. Part of that was because my grandparents were both Native speakers but they had bad experiences through education, taught that their culture was inferior. So they didn't stress the cultural element to my mother. So therefore it wasn't an emphasis in my home. As I got out of my childhood, I made sure that it was something I wanted to learn about and so I went out of my way to get a Native American studies degree just for my own knowledge and information. And through that I started to participate in the Sun Dance ceremonies. I did four years of that, going to more sweat lodges, prayers, and more traditional manner, using sweetgrass when I pray. And some of that stuff was in my home but it wasn't as prevalent as a more traditional Native American household. . . . Our tribal college has language courses and I wanted to take some of those courses and start doing some of that. Actually, one of the things about being back home is that I was hoping to get more involved with traditional culture.

One Montana educator explained how her tribally traditional grandfather encouraged his grandchildren to become culturally assimilated and abandon their tribal language. As an adult, however, she had come to embrace her tribal cultural identity:

> But one thing that I think he was kind of wrong about was that he always told me to try and forget about the old ways because he thought that if I did, I'd be more successful, you know, assimilate more. But I'm learning now that it's actually part of who you are and there's like a balance you try to keep. So that is what I have kind of been trying to do. I really don't know much about ceremonies. I'm learning, you know, because I have some friends who participate in them and my kids have been into sweats and I try to encourage them.

Although most of the educators reported admiration for their tribal cultural heritage and a desire to learn more, not all of them did. Two of the participants expressed ambivalent attitudes toward traditional tribal culture. For instance, a Montana educator explained,

> Not a lot of us have that tie to traditional culture. . . . I didn't have a really strong spiritual base, I don't know a lot of the language, don't know a lot of the customs, traditions, you know. And a lot of our kids don't. I think partly because I wanted it, but there was just nobody there to show me the way. . . . You are sort of stuck in the middle of everything, you know? And you don't really know which way to go. So that's tough—I mean, it's tough because I think people are really hesitant about which way is the way to go, traditional or nontraditional. . . . And that cycle continues because parents, like myself, are sort of stuck in that mode. The kids are stuck in that mode, you know, we are all just kind of stuck. We are all sort of waiting for some big movement to come through and infect us all with this notion of tradition, but I don't think it is ever going to come.

These views notwithstanding, most of the educators evidenced genuine respect for tribal culture. Indeed, most believed closer identification with tribal traditions will lead to greater academic success for students and a reduction in the social problems besetting reservation communities.

Pathway into Education

The participants became educators in a variety of ways. Some knew at an early age they wanted to serve in a reservation school. Others came to a career in education after a long, personal journey. The educators identified two prevailing pathways into their vocation: a direct path and an indirect path. By a direct path, I mean that the participant took a rather conventional route toward a career as an educator. The direct path is characterized by entry into the profession at an early age with few other occupational experiences, whereas an indirect path refers to entry into the profession later in life after a number of career and personal experiences. While a significant number of the participants described following a direct path into their profession, most of them had chosen an indirect path. Indeed, the average age at entry into the education profession for the entire sample was thirty years old.

While many of the respondents who followed a direct path related remarkable personal stories of perseverance and tenacity in order to complete college, their entry into a career in education is typical of many American educators. For instance, these individuals generally decided early in their lives or during college to become an educator, frequently majored in education as an undergraduate student, and gained a position soon after graduation from college. Nine of the twenty-one participants described a direct path toward their vocation.

Analysis of the interviews revealed several interesting features about the nine educators who followed a direct path. First, five of the nine facilitative educators followed a direct path in contrast to only four of the twelve affinitive educators. Second, among the nine participants who chose a direct path, four were second-generation educators. This compares to only one second-generation educator among the twelve participants following an indirect path.

Entry into the classroom upon completion of college at a young age constitutes the most distinctive feature of those taking a direct path. Even for those individuals who did not major in education as an undergraduate student, subsequent to college they quickly decided to seek a career as an educator. Therefore, these individuals did not pursue other career options before becoming a teacher. The examples of an elementary principal from Montana and a South Dakota high school teacher illustrate the direct path into an educational career.

The educator from Montana did not major in education but became a teacher upon college graduation. As a third-generation educator, he entered the profession clearly aware of the demands placed on reservation educators. He described his decision to become a teacher:

> I grew up in this community. I went to school here, K through 12. I went to the University of Montana, got a degree [in a health science field]. I decided not to apply to the professional school, and got married and went into teaching. My grandmother was a teacher, my dad was a teacher, my brother is a teacher, my uncle is a teacher. So it was one of those things that just kind of felt natural. . . . I was married, I had a baby

on the way, and I needed to get a job. And like I said, education was just one of those things that I thought, "Okay, I can do this." Both my wife and I were in the same field and we both went out and got a job. That's where we both started, and been teaching ever since.

The South Dakota teacher, a second-generation educator, majored in education and assumed a position in the school in which she had student taught. Regarding her decision to become a teacher and serve on the reservation, she recounted,

> I student taught here. Once I realized that I was going to go into education, just by coincidence, I decided to student teach here.... I knew some of the faculty here. So I thought it would be a good way for me to learn the ropes knowing some of the people here. I got here and didn't think I was going to like it, and by the end of my student teaching experience, was offered a job and never left. And I can't imagine teaching anywhere else. If I were to leave here, I don't know that I would stay in education.

Several individuals indicated that previous American Indian teachers significantly impacted their decisions to go into education. For instance, on his decision to major in education and become a teacher, a South Dakota educator said, "I knew ... I was going to be a teacher, an educator. I had some very good [American Indian] teachers, pretty good role models. In fact I remember my principal at [name of reservation school] and I remember some of my [American Indian] teachers at [name of reservation school], so that had a big influence on me."

A Montana principal credited former American Indian teachers for his success. This individual emphasized the importance of their example as role models: "Two of the most influential people in my life were two former teachers who both were Native teachers. Being that they kind of conquered the big world off the reservation gave me hope that I could conquer the big world off the reservation, too. But they are still my really good friends and if it wasn't for them I don't know if I would have made it. I don't know if I could have made it."

A Montana teacher noted the importance of attending her state's American Indian Education Committee while still a high school student: "I got involved in our Indian Education Committee and then I was their student representative. So they sent our student reps to different conferences, like out of the state, and I got to meet with all these other students that were interested in education, future teachers or whatever. And then I also got to meet other Indians that were also teachers, older people. I think as a young kid it made me proud to see somebody who was like me, teaching and being successful."

As I considered the nature of the interviews, I realized a distinct and critical feature characterized the descriptions offered by the participants who took a direct path into the classroom: their accounts demonstrate the influence of other educators in their career choice. They came from families of educators or they identified important teachers that had an impact on them. These types of influences are generally absent in the descriptions offered by the participants who followed an indirect path. In fact, several of those individuals specifically related negative experiences with schools and teachers that, at least for a time, served to dissuade them from pursuing education as a profession. It is little wonder why so many of the respondents described their responsibilities in terms of being a role model. For good or for ill, they personally understood the impact teachers have on the lives of Native children.

Most of the educators in this sample—twelve out of the twenty-one—took an indirect path into the field of education. This generally meant the participant did not become an educator until later in life and after a number of significant personal and occupational experiences. Often these individuals either did not major in education as an undergraduate student or, if they did, they enrolled in college at an older age.

A variety of motivations lay behind their decisions to become teachers. Some sought a way to contribute to the reservation in a meaningful and direct fashion. A South Dakota teacher put it like this: "I took education [at the tribal college] because I liked working with children and there was such a high turnover rate of teachers here on the reservation that it was like, we need to have somebody that's from here who will stay here and be with our students." For a few of the respondents, teaching presented a convenient career choice whereby they did not have to uproot family from their homes. Some of the participants gravitated into the classroom after holding other jobs in the school system. In fact, four of the educators began as teachers' aides before obtaining a bachelor's degree and becoming certified teachers. Still others held positions less likely to lead to the classroom. For instance, one South Dakota teacher began her affiliation with the school as a bus driver, while a Montana educator started as one of the school's custodians. The Montana teacher's story reveals how spontaneous, if not unusual, events can transpire and lead to a career as a classroom teacher:

> Well, she [name of teacher's wife] got a job there [at the tribal school] and we moved back. And my intentions were to go to [name of college]. So that summer they needed custodians at the school to work for the summer. So I said, "Oh yeah, I can do that." So I put in my application and sure enough, they hired me. So it got to be more than just a summer job. They said, "Hey, you're pretty good at swinging a mop." "Oh, you betcha." Because I was always taught if you want anything in life you got to work for it, no one is going to give it to you. So I worked there for a while and school was starting and it so happens they were short a substitute. And they were looking all over and didn't have no subs. So they said, "Hey, what time do you get off?" And I said, "I'm off here at noon." "You want to watch this class for the afternoon?" "Me?" You know I was used to picking up after rug-rats in the lunchroom and all that. So it was a kindergarten class. So I subbed that first time, my first interaction with students in our kindergarten classroom. And I liked it. So they said, "There's a tutor job open. Would you want to put in for it?" So I put in for it and I got that. So I started out in kindergarten. I worked in kindergarten for six years. Oh, I loved it. The school district mandated all tutors get their associate's [degree] at least. So I start going to school again and it didn't take me long . . . you know with my prior schooling. . . . After that [receiving his teacher's certification] I was good to go, so I stayed in kindergarten for about six years. And then they moved me up to fourth grade, and finally fifth grade.

At least four participants had not graduated from high school but instead had earned a GED. This fact obviously impacted their pathway into education. For instance, a South Dakota teacher described her dramatic journey into the teaching profession. She began teaching her tribal language at the local college and eventually was invited to teach traditional language subjects to middle school children:

> I went to school and got my education up to the seventh grade and went into a Catholic school and really struggled living in a non-Native world. Moving from a reservation we were different. . . . I ended up with two children at twenty years old and was married for twenty-three years and in the process I didn't have an education because I quit in the seventh grade. . . . So I went back and got a GED. . . . I am sure the Creator was looking out for me because I only went to seventh grade and I had no idea what I was doing getting a GED. But I got the GED and then we had a private college and started in and my very first semester I got a 4.0! [Laughs.] But I really worked at it. I understood that we lived in an impoverished area. I mean, I may not have really understood the terminology at that time, but I knew we lived in a very poor area here. Rich in other ways because you have your kinship, you have your relatives, but in other ways very poor. . . . I did some substitute teaching there at [name of the university] for one of

the [tribal] language teachers. . . . And then I became interested in linguistics being that I am a fluent speaker and kind of had a good feel of it and the passion of it was something that resonated. I was asked to come back here to teach at [name of the tribal college]. . . . So I would work in the summer as an immersion teacher. So I have had a lot of years of teaching children. It's my passion. I feel like it is really important.

Four of the individuals recounted significant negative experiences during their youth that ultimately influenced their career path. All of the events occurred while attending reservation schools and each case involved non-Native teachers. These incidents at first dissuaded them from educational success, but as the participants matured their previous experiences served as motivation for becoming an educator. The episodes revealed the incomprehensible insensitivity they endured as schoolchildren, and the pain of the memories clearly still resonated during the interviews. A Montana teacher related her experiences as a student in a high school math class:

> Why I wanted to get into education was because when I was in high school a certain teacher told me I wasn't any good in math. I mean [the teacher] made a thing about it. "Let [participant's name] go to the board and show us!" And laugh! I was devastated. "I know I'm not any good, but help me!" So I kind of stayed away from math subjects and just did the basics of what I had to get out of high school. But I decided that, "I think I'm a little smarter than that." So when I went back to school, I did pretty well. I had to work at it, but I did well. And so I thought, "You know, I'm going to be the kind of teacher that's going to help somebody, not put them down and say mean things to them. I want them to know they can do it" . . . I was scared then [during high school]. I'm not good at math, I thought. But as I had my own kids later on, I was helping them with their schoolwork and I was thinking, "Shoot, I can do this and I like it."

The participant's self-confidence eventually overcame the initial ridicule she endured as a high school student. Today she is a highly respected and successful middle school math teacher. In an even more dramatic (and ironic) example, a South Dakota elementary principal described the following experience:

> When I was in third grade, there were no Indian teachers. Just cooks and support staff. But the teacher, she had us get up in front of the room and tell what we were going to be when we grew up. So we did. And I got up and told her that I was going to be a teacher and I was going to come back to [name of the elementary school]. And she told me there was no such thing as Indian teachers. I cried! I went running out and thank God my grandpa was a bus driver and my grandmother was the cook. So I went right

to my grandmother in the kitchen and she went and found my grandpa. Needless to say, I felt sorry for that poor teacher. He told her, "My granddaughter can be anything she wants to be and when she comes back she is going to run this school."

This participant fulfilled her grandfather's prophetic pronouncement when years later she did indeed assume the principal's position at that very same elementary school. Despite the inspiring ability of these individuals to overcome discouraging events, it is nevertheless disturbing to consider that the offensive conduct of teachers could have cost these two reservations valuable educators. One wonders how many others have been lost to reservation schools due to similar attitudes and behavior.

Academic Training and Nature of the Careers

The participants came from a variety of academic backgrounds, but the most common academic training among them was a major in education. Fourteen majored in education as an undergraduate. All but one held bachelor's degrees (one held an associate's degree and was certified by the tribe and state as a culture and language teacher), but all were certified as teachers or principals. Additionally, eleven of the participants held master's degrees. Although three indicated they planned to pursue doctoral work, none had a doctorate.

Tribal colleges played a significant role in the careers of the participants. Eleven of the twenty-one educators attended a tribal college either as an undergraduate or as a graduate student. Tribal colleges were especially instrumental for older individuals who followed an indirect path. Indeed, several related experiences similar to those expressed by a Montana teacher:

> I went to [name of an off-reservation university] right out of high school. . . . And then I got married and we came back here and I raised my kids and when they got into school I thought, "I think I will go back to school." Because we lived on one income and it was kind of hard. But I made that decision to stay at home with my kids so I could pick them up after school. And as they were all in school, I'm like, "Okay, I think I will go back." So I started here [at the tribal college], which really helped. If it wasn't here I probably wouldn't have went. I mean, I know I wouldn't have, because I wouldn't have left my family.

Most of the educators had spent their entire careers serving reservation schools. A second-generation educator from South Dakota who had never taught off the reservation stated, "I grew up in Native education. It kind of runs in my blood." Six of the twenty-one educators had previously taught in nonreservation schools, but only one had spent the majority of his career off the reservation. Another educator's career was about equally divided between schools on and off reservations.

Affinitive educators and facilitative educators evidenced few differences in their academic training and nature of their careers. Compared to affinitive educators, facilitative educators were a little more likely to hold an undergraduate degree from an off-reservation school. Also, not surprising given their tendency to follow an indirect path into a career in education, affinitive educators were more likely than facilitative educators to have taken an undergraduate degree from a tribal college. However, no real difference appears among those with graduate degrees. Moreover, there is no discernible difference between the two types of educators in regards to the types of schools and communities served during their careers. Most of both the affinitive and facilitative educators had spent their careers largely in service to reservation schools.

Career Goals

Teacher retention represents a major problem facing the nation's schools. According to Alan Dessoff (2010), in the coming decade tens of thousands of educators will leave the profession each year, most due to retirement. The attrition of veteran teachers will hit rural school districts with high poverty rates especially hard. Unfortunately, the situation for rural school districts has become even more acute under NCLB's tightly defined high-quality teacher provision (Eppley, 2009; Hill & Barth, 2004). Indeed, demographic and educational policy developments have combined to create a particularly troublesome state of affairs for reservation schools (Erickson et al., 2008; Ward, 2005). Given this context, I wanted to know if the participants planned to leave the profession. One of the most common reasons why individuals report they leave teaching is general job dissatisfaction (Erickson et al., 2008). With that in mind, I was interested in whether they regretted becoming a teacher.

Remarkably, only one of the participants related outright regret in his career choice, but the unique circumstances and timing of the interview undoubtedly influenced his responses to my inquiries. This educator's school had suffered through a series of student suicides. The aftermath of these tragedies had created enormous emotional strain.

Most of the participants were well established as veteran educators, and indicated plans to remain in their profession. Only two of the educators voiced ambivalent feelings about their decisions to become an educator. Even in these cases, however, each individual resolved his or her ambivalence by emphasizing the satisfaction derived from serving as an educator. For instance, when I asked about any regret in becoming an educator, a South Dakota principal reflected,

> Some days, I think about how I would do in the business world. I had a dream of being a lawyer or doing something like that. But generally overall in the last twenty-two years of being in education, I'm pretty happy with where I've been and where I'm going. I still have some big goals. I want to get my specialist [degree] some time. I'm still young enough and maybe [could] go on and get a doctorate and do some of those things. I never stop thinking about where I need to be at the next level professionally. I don't know if I'm going to get there, I really don't. But I like the situation that I'm in now because I'm not only trying to improve students' lives, but I think I'm learning a lot in this position.

Not only did the majority of the educators have no regrets, but many of them emphatically declared they had selected an appropriate career path for themselves. A Montana elementary explained, "No. No, I don't regret becoming a teacher at all. I love my job. I love working in education and I love working with young people. I love having discussions with teachers and talking about big-picture things. I love having my summers off, too. [Laughs.]"

A few of the participants discussed their desire to assume leadership positions within the school or district. For example, while discussing her long-range career plans, a Montana teacher stated she would leave the classroom only for an administrative leadership position:

> No. No, I don't [have any regrets about becoming an educator]. And I don't think I have even peaked yet. . . . The only way I would leave is probably to be an administrator. I never wanted us [the school] to become a swinging door. We were so stable here for so long. But there have been so many changes in the last three to five years. If I were asked and it was something that could make things better, I would do it. To make sure our school survives, I would do it. Because I am committed here. This is the only place I will work until retirement so I would. But it wouldn't be leaving the school. If I could serve our students better and make things better, I would.

I also wanted to know if the participants had any plans to leave their current positions or perhaps the field of education entirely. Although only one individual expressed regret in becoming a teacher, three of the educators did indicate either a desire or the actual intention to relocate and leave their present position. One individual had accepted a position as an administrator in another reservation community. Another related she planned to leave her teaching position within a few more years in order to pursue another opportunity, and would most likely leave the reservation. One of the younger educators related he had already informed his school administrators about his intention to leave within a few years. Nevertheless, he outlined his intention to remain active in American Indian education:

> Going to another community is definitively an option. . . . My wife is making a sacrifice for me to be here. And my family is here. So I think at some point down the road I will definitively need to make the same sacrifice and we have already discussed this. I've talked to my administration that I am not going to be here forever. I will be here for a while but she is a long way from home and I think at some point we will be in an area that's closer to her home. When I'm doing that, I still want to stay involved here. That's why I think I like curriculum development because it will give me the opportunity to stay involved and working in professional development and things like that. It will give me opportunities to go to communities like this and maybe do some training and things I've learned and things I will learn eventually.

Two other educators discussed their concern with the deteriorating nature of their community. Both of these educators were from the same reservation and served the same school. Unfortunately, they believed that a move to a community off the reservation might be necessary for the sake of their respective families. They also understood such a move would likely necessitate they leave their present positions. With a great deal of regret in his voice, one of the educators explained why he would move to a community off the reservation: "[If] our community starts to fall apart more than it has. The school has improved since I have been here, but the community has gone down. If the community were to continue that downward spiral, that's one of the things. And that's more for my family and kids than it is for me."

Dessoff's (2010) warning about problems resulting from pending retirements has special relevancy. The average age of the participants in this study was forty-seven, with an average of eighteen years of experience. Six of the participants were fifty-four years or older. A number of them discussed their plans for upcoming retirement. Many of these individuals held positions of significant leadership, and a number were fluent tribal language speakers. Reservation schools will likely find it difficult to replace individuals such as these. Although too humble to admit it, they seemed to realize their value to the reservation, and they typically expressed regret and some reluctance about retirement. Only one individual related that the mounting frustrations of serving as an educator made retirement increasingly welcomed.

Simply based on the accounts offered, it is possible that a remarkable attrition may occur among this sample of American Indian educators. Consider that of the twenty-one participants six will retire in the coming decade and at least two indicated plans to assume other positions outside reservation schools. Conservatively, eight of the American Indian educators I interviewed may not be serving reservation schools in the next few years. This would be a loss of more than one-third of the participants. Moreover, I have not even included the two educators who believed they may have to leave the reservation for the good of their families. Of course, one cannot generalize this pattern beyond this particular sample. Given the fact there are few American Indian educators and even fewer educators who are fluent in tribal languages, however, such losses potentially represent a serious issue for reservation schools.

COMPARISON OF AFFINITIVE EDUCATORS AND FACILITATIVE EDUCATORS

Affinitive educators and facilitative educators shared many important personal characteristics. They were generally products of reservations and most frequently served on the reservation of their tribal membership. Many had lived in large urban areas but few could claim sustained residences in metropolitan areas. Nevertheless, they also described a number of prominent differences. In many respects, they diverged in early cultural socialization experiences, they differed in their family history with college education, and they typically had followed different paths into their chosen profession.

Half of the affinitive educators described their early socialization as oriented toward tribal cultural traditions. Indeed, six of the affinitive educators reported fluency in a tribal language. None of the facilitative educators described early socialization experiences oriented toward tribal cultural traditions, and not one of them related fluency in a tribal language.

The two groups of educators also revealed an obvious difference in family history with higher education. The majority of facilitative educators were not the first among their families to graduate from college. In fact, five out of the nine came from families in which a least one parent was a college graduate. This compares to only one of the twelve affinitive educators. Simply put, virtually all the affinitive educators were first-generation college graduates. Moreover, all six of those who described culturally traditional socialization experiences were first-generation college graduates.

Finally, affinitive educators and facilitative educators diverged in the manner in which they had become educators. Whereas most of the facilitative educators (five of the nine) followed a direct path into the profession, the majority of affinitive educators (eight of the twelve) took a more meandering, indirect path. This, of course, generally means the affinitive educators became teachers later in life and were slightly more likely to rely on tribal colleges for their academic preparation.

CONCLUSION

The findings reported in this chapter reveal important differences in the personal, family, and cultural backgrounds of the participants. Affinitive educators frequently described early socialization experiences oriented toward tribal traditions, were first-generation college graduates, and followed an indirect path into their careers. Facilitative educators, on the other hand, tended to relate early socialization oriented either to the mainstream or to somewhere between the mainstream and traditional cultures. These individuals were less likely to be first-generation college graduates and more likely to have pursued a direct path into the classroom. All of these critically important life experiences provide these two types of educators with unique perspectives. It is thus reasonable to assume they also shape the participants' understanding of their profession and the way they defined their roles as American Indian educators.

In the last chapter, I suggested that gender, professional position, and school setting have little to do with how affinitive and facilitative educators came to define their responsibilities. Rather, their personal background accounts for the divergence between the two types of educators. Affinitive educators, who stressed the importance of role modeling and building personal relationships, frequently came from culturally traditional backgrounds. Their conceptions of appropriate responsibilities for educators reflect the expectations typical of their upbringing. Traditionally, a responsible teacher models appropriate behavior and values and thus strives to connect with others in intimate, personal ways. Conversely, facilitative educators were more likely to come from backgrounds oriented toward the cultural mainstream. Frequently, they were exposed to the early influence of significant educators, often were second-generation college graduates, and were a little more likely to report having gone through conventional teacher training programs.

These social, cultural, and professional experiences likely help lead an individual to regard professional competence as the trademark responsibility of an educator.

The existing literature supports this interpretation of the findings. Miller Cleary and Peacock (1998), upon conclusion of their research with sixty Native and non-Native educators serving American Indian children, relate that the personal, cultural, and professional backgrounds of teachers greatly impact their practice. Robert Rhodes (1994) argues educators must understand the unique social, cultural, and learning needs of Native children. Although Rhodes directs much of his discussion toward non-Native educators, he too concludes that personal background characteristics color the way teachers appreciate American Indian education issues. Moreover, he argues that teacher preparation programs commonly train teachers to approach their profession in a mechanical, step-by-step fashion that may not be particularly productive for American Indian children. Rhodes suggests educators assume a facilitator-coach style of teaching that he asserts is more aligned with the learning styles and cultural expectations common to Native students and communities. Most important, he contends any transition in instructional modes requires the educator to critically examine his or her personal and cultural background experiences and resultant expectations. In other words, Rhodes argues the background of teachers shapes the way they define their roles as educators.

Certainly, the sample contains notable homogeneity. The participants were largely rural people with deep connections to reservations. Most had attended reservation schools, many in the same building where they now serve as educators. Based on the insights provided by the interviews, I believe a significant reason why the participants diverged into affinitive educators and facilitative educators is their personal backgrounds and, in particular, their early socialization and later cultural orientation experiences. Simply put, those who reported a traditional, tribal orientation were more inclined to identify the roles associated with affinitive educators as professionally appropriate. Conversely, those who came from a mainstream cultural orientation were more likely to embrace roles defining facilitative educators.

CHAPTER 3

Challenges Are Every Day
Prevailing Challenges Facing the Educators

> *Challenges are every day. Challenges are just getting kids here. Challenges are trying to make sure these kids come in and we got breakfast bars here. A lot of times they don't come with breakfast. Challenges are the parents may be fighting or are the parents even there? Challenges are, Where is the kid going to go at the end of the school day? Make sure he gets home. Is it safe there? We sometimes have to call the cops to make sure it's a safe home. Challenges are every day.* —Montana principal reflecting on dealing with challenges facing reservation schools

The morning was beautiful and clear. I waited in the large staff meeting room located in a doublewide trailer adjacent to the main building. I looked out the window up the hill as the morning breeze kneaded the prairie grass in a gentle swaying dance. The room was quiet and a bit dark. The only light came from the windows lining the trailer, but a hill still partially blocked the bright sun. The participant came into the room; after exchanging introductions and a few pleasantries, we sat in undersized chairs at a large table. The teacher had grown up in this isolated community of the reservation and had served the school for more than twenty years. During that time, she had been everything from bus driver to third grade teacher, her current position. No one could begin to estimate her investment in the children, the school, and the community. We progressed through the interview, eventually arriving at a discussion on the challenges associated with serving as an educator on the reservation. The exchange revealed a raw emotional wound produced by her two decades of service.

> Being where I am from, I know the people. I know the families. The students see that and know that I am from this community. So I think I have more of a bond with them. Even the parents, the students I had at the beginning [of her teaching career], I'm teaching their children now. [Laughs.] It makes you feel older but it's good. You have that respect. They are so cooperative. It's not 100 percent parental involvement, but we're kind of isolated from the communities anyway. A lot of them don't have cars to

> come in or they don't have telephones. Usually it's by notes. But I try to communicate with them. And if a student is absent a lot, I make the phone call and if I can't talk to them I try to go out to their house and see what's going on. Because of alcoholism, a lot of the students have a hard life and it's sad. [She grows very intent and begins to cry.] I'm sorry. [Soon she is weeping.]

Her anguish touched me greatly and I managed a feeble, "Bless your heart." After a long pause to compose, she resumed her thoughts as the tears continued to flow.

> They just have a hard life. It has so many effects from it besides attendance. Because of poverty, no employment, and just stuff like that. And the students can't help it. It's not their fault. But I think it affects them a lot with their learning because they all have this block. It's hard for them to retain information. So it's like reteaching every day. And it's usually around the first of the month that is the hardest for them, I think. I guess they can adjust, but it's hard for them to have parents that drink all weekend and then come to school and be a student, ready to learn. It's hard for them because they are thinking about, "Oh, what's going to happen when I go home today? Is my mom and dad going to be drinking?" So it's really hard for them. But I think that when they are here, it's safe. It's a safe place for them and they get their meals here, two meals anyway. Sometimes, for some of them, that's their only meals. But it's a lot harder because they don't have the experiences that students off the rez might.

Teaching demands a great deal from a person. Even under the most optimal conditions, a career in education requires years of training and then more training, long hours of classroom preparation, tenacity to meet ever-present standards requirements, deftness dealing with a myriad of student learning styles and personalities, flexibility to differentiate instruction, and the ability to communicate and work with parents. To add into this mix complex social conditions that threaten to undermine instruction is enough to demoralize even the most determined educator.

Ultimately, a school cannot escape the prevailing social conditions surrounding it. All of the educators I interviewed served in reservations confronted with perplexing and persistent social problems. Deeply entrenched poverty, chronic unemployment, heartrending child neglect and abuse, domestic violence, disturbingly high rates of auto accidents, and suicides all afflict the five reservations I visited during the research. And, of course, there is also the long-time enemy of alcohol and substance abuse. Little wonder our discussion on the challenges the participants encounter consumed roughly one-third of the total interview time.

FRUSTRATIONS AND PERSEVERANCE

I find it remarkable given the enormity of the challenges facing these educators that they retained their optimism, and faithfully served with extraordinary hope for the future. However, that does not mean the educators soldier on with complete sanguinity. The participants candidly outlined their many frustrations. In fact, most participants spoke with unflinching honesty about their struggles with discouragement. A few of the participants related they were nearing the end of their coping tether. A Montana teacher confided, "I'm tired of trying to work with somebody who has a problem, like they haven't slept or they haven't eaten, or they are doing drugs. It's just that I am tired of it. I am tired of it."

This chapter explores the challenges facing the educators. During the course of the interviews, they related a host of complex, troubling issues. In fact, they identified so many it took quite an effort to systematically analyze the volume of material. Thirteen separate themes emerged from the data analysis. While considering the patterns in the data, I came to realize many of the themes are conceptually connected to one another. For instance, some of the themes relate to general social conditions found on the reservation, while others associate with conditions located within the school system. I grouped these challenges according to the conceptual relationship they have with one another, then created four theoretical constructs to act as a kind of conceptual umbrella, and sorted the thirteen specific themes under them. The four theoretical constructs are reservation social conditions, attitudes toward education, student-related issues, and school staff issues.

Reservation Social Conditions

Reservation social conditions relate to challenges resulting from the general economic and family circumstances of the reservation. The analysis of the interviews revealed three specific dimensions of this theoretical construct: poverty, family dysfunctions, and alcohol and drug abuse. The social problems found on the reservations occupy a prominent place in the concerns of the participants. Indeed, eighteen of the twenty-one participants specifically discussed at least one of the three dimensions of reservation social conditions as a serious challenge to their efforts as educators.

Challenges associated with poverty create persistent difficulties for the participants. More of the educators (sixteen of the twenty-one educators) identified poverty as a challenge than any other single issue. Both affinitive educators and facilitative educators displayed similar concerns over this challenge. Nine of the affinitive educators and seven of the facilitative educators described difficulties associated with the impoverished conditions of the reservation.

The participants have first-hand experience with the harmful effects of poverty in their students' lives. Time and again, their stories revealed the severity of its consequences. In particular, they were quick to point out how acutely poverty impedes students' potential to learn. Expressing frustration in the failure of some of the teachers in her district to appreciate the desperate condition of many students' lives, a Montana principal explained,

> We can say, "Oh yeah, they come from a home where parents are drinking all the time," but I understand that because I lived it. . . . And I know what it's like to go a day without eating food because there's not enough. So, I totally understand that. Well, you know what? They're dirty because they don't have a washing machine, or they're dirty because their water got turned off, or their electricity was turned off because they didn't pay the bills. . . . So I guess I have that empathy because I've lived it. But I'll tell you. I went up to some of the homes here and I didn't realize how poverty-stricken some of them are. Because some homes I would go into and there'd be no furniture. There would be a mattress in the living room and that's where they ate, that's where they slept. . . . But I just think as a teacher, or as teachers, they're saying, "Well, why don't they bring their homework back?" We need to understand where they're coming from. Homework is not a top priority for a lot of kids.

A South Dakota principal also reflected on how basic human needs, frequently neglected because of impoverished living conditions, take primacy over learning, "There are many [challenges] that I see here. Poverty is huge here. Students come hungry and poorly dressed and things like that. You know all about Maslow's hierarchy—well, we got to take care of those needs first before any learning can take place. And that's a huge issue here on the reservation. We're fully aware of what we face. But I would say that is the biggest issue."

Similarly, a Montana teacher said of the poverty on her reservation, "I believe the challenge, number one, is the poverty. And with the poverty come a lot of challenges in itself. I think that some of our people are more concerned with getting something to eat, getting bills paid. Education—I really believe that education on the hierarchy structure for our Native people is not at the top of the structure."

Despite their frustrations, many of the educators remained optimistic that their efforts can affect change in the lives of severely impoverished children.

One South Dakota educator displayed indignation over the suggestion that social conditions such as poverty might prevent the educational success of her students. She explained how attending the local tribal college helped clarify the history of her tribe, and how she came to a dramatic epiphany resulting in a career as a teacher:

> It was kind of like a healing, learning about my history and learning about who I was, where I came from, and what had happened. And I thought our people are in this hole and are angry and I learned how to come out of that anger and move forward and get my education and not blame my failures or my weaknesses on what the government did to us or what happened in the past. I needed to move forward and do that for myself and my kids. And when I started realizing how hurting our people were, how we depend on monthly checks, ADC food, and food stamps, and stuff like that, I wanted to get into the classroom and teach the kids. People say, "Oh these people, they are poverty stricken. The poor kids. They are so poor they can't learn." That's not true! I wanted to prove to my people and show the parents of these kids that there is nothing that should be holding anybody back!

This educator's optimism is laudable. She displayed a confident attitude necessary to assist children to overcome oppressive social and personal circumstances. Most of the participants would likely agree with her. They believed in their students and embraced the conviction that people can surmount daunting circumstances working against them. Indeed, many of the participants had overcome those same circumstances themselves.

Family dysfunctions, a second dimension of reservation social conditions, constitute a major challenge for the educators. Fourteen of the educators identified family dysfunctions as a serious obstacle. In fact, the majority of both affinitive educators (seven out of twelve) and facilitative educators (seven out of nine) described challenges resulting from the family circumstances of their students. Most frequently, these concerns included domestic violence and child neglect. Unfortunately, the stark poverty found on the reservation tends to magnify family difficulties; the accounts offered by the respondents reveal the intersection between poverty and family dysfunctions. The educators, such as a Montana principal, offered vivid descriptions of desperate family circumstances: "As a teacher, I took it [teaching] very seriously because that was my job. I have to teach them how to do this. I had to know my material so that I could teach it to them. But, I also needed to have that understanding they might not understand this today because their mom and dad were up late last night fighting. Dad's sitting in jail right now; mom's in the hospital. What's more important here?" After careful reflection, another Montana principal noted,

> Well I think from the very moment when babies are born they need to be loved, they need to be cherished, they need parents giving that kid the best life that the kid can have, keeping drugs and alcohol away from the home and being supportive of the kid their whole life. And it's free. It doesn't cost money. Not leaving the kid sitting in the chair in front of the TV with a bottle strapped to its mouth. Not neglecting the kid to the point where your kid gets taken from the home. Those things happen every day. Every day they happen here. It's so simple, you know? We can only do so much. When that kid goes home, they need a home that's safe, and a home that's conducive to a warm and nurturing lifestyle.

Alcohol and drug abuse is a serious social problem on the reservations where this research occurred. Almost half of the participants (ten out of twenty-one) mentioned alcohol and drug abuse as a challenge. More specifically, five of the affinitive educators and five of the facilitative educators indicated concern over this issue. A Montana principal believed alcohol and drug use is so prevalent among the youth of his reservation that such use has become routinized. When asked about the challenges he faces as an educator he answered, "The encountering of the drugs and alcohol at a much younger level than I would say off the reservation. And the acceptance of the drinking and the drugs. I hear it all the time, 'Everybody drinks, everybody does drugs. That's what you do here on the rez.' I almost call it the 'reservation culture' because they are taking on [an attitude of] this is how they are supposed to act. And those are the biggest challenges, I think. To try to fight through those."

Another Montana educator's comments suggest the heartbreaking tragedy resulting from this social problem: "We need to come face to face with the problem of the alcohol abuse, the prescription pill use, the methamphetamine use, and we're just starting to now see the results of that with children that are coming into the school. And, so, working with children that have been fetal-affected by those is a challenge."

Clearly, poverty, family dysfunctions, and alcohol and drug abuse constitute serious challenges for the participants. It is important to bear in mind that these are also deeply entrenched problems, and recent evidence suggests that social conditions are not improving (Willeto, 2007; Yu & Stiffman, 2007). One source estimates that 60 percent of South Dakota American Indian children live in homes where no parent has full-time, year-round employment and that more than 60 percent live in single-parent families (Willeto, 2007). Despite the devastating consequences of alcohol abuse in Native communities, there has been a general relaxing of tribal prohibitions against alcohol sales due in large part to the emergence of reservation gaming (Kovas, McFarland, Landen, Lopez, & May, 2008). The future will reveal the impact of such policy developments on reservation communities (Berman, 2002).

It is nearly impossible to untangle the intersections between poverty, family dysfunctions, and alcohol and drug abuse. What is certain is that Native children residing in healthy homes are less likely to fall victim to impoverished conditions and substance abuse. One study comparing Montana Native and non-Native youths found that American Indian young people consume alcohol and engage in heavy episodic drinking at rates much higher than white youths (Friese, Grube, Seninger, Paschall, & Moore, 2011). However, other studies reveal that positive family relationships and strong value systems mitigate such behaviors among Native youth (Lonczak, Fernandez, Austin, Marlatt, & Donovan, 2007; Yu & Stiffman, 2010). The educators I met certainly intuitively understood these dynamics. Indeed, they witnessed them at work every day.

Attitudes Toward Education

A general lack of regard for education perplexed the participants. Many of the educators described general indifference to education and schools as commonplace on the reservation. Others related their frustrations with the reluctance of families to support the education of children. Interestingly, a few also spoke of pressures derived from community expectations placed on American Indian teachers. I identified three dimensions that cluster around a theoretical construct I refer to simply as attitudes toward education. These dimensions include community indifference, lack of family support, and community scrutiny on American Indian educators. Sixteen of the educators discussed at least one of the dimensions included under the theoretical construct of attitudes toward education.

Most of the participants described the challenge resulting from community indifference toward education. Thirteen of the educators (including six of the affinitive educators and seven of the facilitative educators) expressed concerns ranging from irritation to alarm over community indifference to education. Eventually, many students appropriate this disposition themselves. As a Montana educator recounted, "The challenges right now, I would say, for whatever reason our community doesn't see education as important. They just don't. I have had kids tell me, 'I don't need this because even if I don't get a job I still get paid.' Those types of comments really become a challenge."

Other educators reflected on the context behind the apathy within the community. These individuals understood many Native people harbor resentment toward schools as a result of personal and historic negative experiences. While a few acknowledged a slow change in attitudes, a reluctance to embrace the mission of reservation schools persists. A South Dakota teacher reflected,

> I can understand. As a Native teacher, as a Native myself, as a product of watching my mom and my grandfather who went to Carlisle Indian School. My mother went to the boarding school system. And going through a boarding school myself, just for a couple of years, and I hated it. But I can see why they don't care for education. They don't support education because what they did during that time. Taking the kids and forcing them to go. Education wasn't good for them at that time. We have a long way to go and parents are starting to see that education is important. But education was very detrimental to the Native culture and family unit. So I can understand that.

In the estimation of one Montana educator, American Indian educators have a special responsibility to counter the indifference toward education common to many reservation communities:

> It's more of indifference, I guess. . . . And I think there are groups on the reservation who think that, and their kids come to school with that attitude. And it's up to the educators in that school to change that mentality. And I think a lot of that stems from the early education of Native people and the boarding school system and the loss of language and culture where it was a negative experience for our elders, for some of them. And it taught them not to value education because it wasn't important because there was a negative connection to education.

The majority of the educators reported frustration with a lack of family support for education, the second dimension of attitudes toward education. Twelve of the respondents (seven of the affinitive educators and five of the facilitative educators) discussed the reluctance of families to support the education of their children. A South Dakota principal explained it simply:

> Parents don't see it [education] as a viable path. I mean, some parents just feel that you get to eighth grade and you're done. If you can get that far, that's great. There's probably a mixture of those kinds of people who think that way and I think there are some who value education and really believe that if you want to be successful you need to go

on and get an education. A lot of our kids turn to the armed forces for success. But I don't think we are there yet as far as parents valuing education.

A Montana principal related his efforts to combat family indifference toward his school. While he acknowledged the context for the diffidence among some reservation parents, he also emphasized the critical importance of parental involvement in the educational success of students:

> There's still this reluctance for parents to be involved in their kids' education. And I understand that maybe they've had bad experiences with school and their grandparents have had bad experiences with the school. But I think it's so complicated. People say, "Well, parents need to be more involved in the school. So offer up a parent-teacher night and invite them in." But it's way more complicated than that. I think the school, a lot of times, is seen as the big evil force that either flunks or retains kids, and that's it. That's pretty much all we're known for by some parents. . . . Parental involvement, a lot of our kids don't have it. But it's one of those factors of success with their lives. . . . I wish the parents could see the worth in their involvement in their kids' education. Because the kids want it and they need it but some parents are so busy drinking and doing other things that it doesn't mean a lot to them.

A Montana elementary teacher outlined the convergence of a number of challenges that, in his view, results in parental indifference toward the education of their children:

> Some parents don't teach their kids to come to school every day and make sure that they are listening. We have abuse problems at home. We have kids where, for some of them, school is a safe place where they are fed on a regular basis, they are not hit. Those are challenges that we have where some of these kids have really negative home environments. . . . The importance of education isn't stressed and that makes it difficult sometimes to teach these kids when it's not being reinforced. You can tell the difference between the homes where education is a priority and the homes where there is apathy towards education. You know, school is just a place to drop off the kids for a while in some houses. The opportunity isn't realized by those parents.

A few participants described another peculiar, albeit disconcerting, tendency for some families to actively discourage the academic success of their children. Certainly, an inclination to discourage the educational advancement of one's own children involves immense social and emotional complexities. The participants attributed such attitudes to psychological trauma resulting from entrenched poverty combined with emotional pathologies related to alcohol and drug use. A Montana principal reflected, "I've encountered where parents don't want their kids to succeed, which has always baffled me. But they tell them that if somehow they get a better education or things that they would feel that they were better than their parents. I have actually heard the comment, 'You think you're better than me?' And those types of things are a big challenge here."

A Montana middle school teacher recounted a revealing episode that illustrates the emotional drama involved when parents discourage their children from realizing the opportunities afforded by educational achievement. Her perplexity over the episode still resonated as she told her story:

> The tribe got rid of the requirement to have a high school diploma or a GED to work for our tribe. And I thought that was crazy. And my students thought that was crazy. So we decided to write a letter telling why we thought that was not smart. And so my students wrote letters. Some of their mothers, they had been really young mothers, and they had gotten mad at their daughters for writing these letters and saying, "You think you are better than me?" And one of the girls, I remember her telling me, "My mom got mad at me and said, 'I'm doing fine, you think you're better than me?'" Another girl said, her mom said that since she hangs out with me she thinks she's a white girl, a prep girl, and just makes fun of her.

Another Montana principal spoke to the reasons he believed some parents attempt to undermine the educational success of their children. In his view, parents discourage the academic achievement of their children due to deeply intertwined personal and social circumstances:

> I think one of the things that, if you have ever read any of Ruby Payne's work on poverty, there is a part that talks about assets and as Native people we don't have a lot of things. We don't surround ourselves with a lot of things, cars, houses. But the one thing that they can hold to, the one thing that they truly cherish, is the kids. Even to the point where they don't want their kids to go. It's the only thing they have and this is the thing they want to hold on to, the one possession that they don't want to see go and be successful. Well, I think they want them to be successful, but I think there is a big fear of them leaving and not coming back. And I think another part of it is there's a whole big drug and alcohol thing that I haven't touched on. . . . But the possession thing. I can really relate to that because I see that a lot. The people, the grandparents, don't want their kids to go because this is the only "thing" that they have that they can call their own. And have it go and be successful and maybe not come back is in some ways unacceptable.

The participants recognized the power and significance of role models in their communities. The educators were also conscious of the responsibilities that go along with serving in such a public capacity. Thus, the community scrutiny on American Indian educators is a third dimension of attitudes toward education. Seven educators spoke of the pressure they felt because of the attention on them. Perhaps not surprisingly given their emphasis on serving as a role model, six of those seven individuals were affinitive educators. A Montana elementary teacher expressed her concern over the scrutiny on Native educators:

> There are two other teachers who are Native American that have worked here longer than I. And I think they really enjoy their teaching but I think they would probably say the same thing about the pressure of being a role model. And when your family has problems, say my daughter or sons have problems, you feel like, "Oh, they did something terrible and everyone is not going to think the same of me because they're my children and I raised them and what was I teaching them?" And that type of thing. Which doesn't necessarily mean that it's your problem. I mean, that you were the cause of the problem. But that's what a lot of people would think.

A Montana principal also discussed an awareness of being closely observed by students and others in the community. For this educator, such scrutiny simply comes with the responsibilities of his position: "That's a tall order because you always have to watch who is watching you and make sure that you are doing exactly what you told the kids. That's one of the things they do not stand for, is that it's okay for you to tell me something as long as you follow that. But if you're not following that I'm not going to hear you at all."

Much like the Montana principal quoted above, several of the participants' comments indicate they regarded community scrutiny as a natural part of serving the reservation. For example, a Montana high school teacher related, "When I see kids out in the community, I think they respect me. And one thing my husband and I have always said is that we don't use alcohol, of course we don't use drugs. Even if we were social drinkers, I would never, ever, be in a bar near this area and be afraid that you were going to see your own students or their parents. So we have always set that precedent for ourselves."

It is hard to imagine a situation more laden with irony than American Indian education. On the one hand, federal and state policies used schools to force cultural assimilation. The misuse of this social institution bears much of the responsibility for the devastating cultural loss and family dysfunction among Native peoples. Consequently, generations of American Indians came to regard education with deep distrust and resentment—feelings, it should be noted, that are still widely held on many reservations today. On the other hand, education offers critically important prospects for personal betterment and community development. Simply put, the requirements of postmodern society demand an educationally prepared population, including a reservation population. Regarding the crucial importance of formal education to the well-being of Native peoples, I have previously written as follows:

> The enduring issues of the past will constitute the pressing concerns of the present and future for Native peoples. Sovereignty, community revitalization, language preservation, rights of identity and self-definition, land use and management, the list can go on, are among the most compelling issues. The complexity of concerns reflects the ever-increasing intricacy of the world in which we inhabit. American Indian leaders face daunting challenges. The demands confronting Native peoples are all tied in one way or another to educational issues. Certainly grounding in Native wisdom is essential to answer these challenges. So, too, preparation to meet the demands of postmodern society is needed. (Huffman, 2010, p. 231)

The educators in this study certainly understand the importance of education to meet personal and community challenges. As a result, both affinitive and facilitative educators voiced frustration over the apathy toward education found on the reservation in general and among Native families in particular. The only real difference between the two types of educators is found in their perception on the community scrutiny on Native educators. Clearly, the affinitive educators displayed a greater sensitivity on this issue than the facilitative educators. However, such a disposition among affinitive educators is understandable. They regard their most important function to be a role model. It would be surprising if they did not recognize that serving as a role model includes the close examination by students as well as the larger community.

Student-Related Issues

Student-related issues involve challenges ranging from student misbehavior, to problematic attitudes, to personal tragedies. I identified three themes associated with this theoretical construct: discipline problems, academic apathy, and student suicides. Fifteen of the twenty-one respondents referred to challenges associated with at least one of these themes.

The discipline problems among students create distress to the extent that eleven of the participants described such behavior as a challenge. There does appear to be a difference in perception on this issue. Whereas seven of the nine facilitative educators reported concerns over disciplinary issues, only four of the twelve affinitive educators related similar concerns. Put another way, almost all the facilitative educators but fewer than half of the affinitive educators discussed disciplinary problems as a challenge they face. A Montana teacher indicated the disciplinary problems have gotten worse in recent years: "There are other challenges in a child's life, you know, just behavioral issues. It seems like, I don't know, in the last several years it really seems to be a lot of behavioral issues with our young people. I don't know if it's the family structure, you know, how intact it is. But then the family structure has changed so much these days, to one it might seem intact."

A South Dakota high school teacher compared her challenges with the classroom management issues facing teachers in nonreservation schools. For this educator much of the problems displayed by her students stem from deep emotional issues:

> There is a lot of depression with our kids. They are not the normal depression signs like withdrawal. A lot of it is getting in trouble. We don't know if there are other things going on at home or things that are bothering them here and they are not addressing it with us, so it comes out as defiance. They're roaming the halls, they're getting in trouble, they're swearing at teachers, and it's getting at the root of the problem when we don't have enough staff to figure out what that is. . . . Classroom management in public school [off the reservation] is minimal, it really is minimal. I mean, it is getting them to hand their homework in, to quiet down when you start class. We don't leave the classroom for the first two months because you have ADHD, and you have this kid is still smoking and he needs a smoke right now, and this kid who is mad at his girlfriend and she is roaming the halls looking for him right now and he knows it. There are all these things going on and you do classroom management first and then you do teaching. And it's the opposite in other schools. You teach and then you might have to do a little classroom management.

Like many educators, a number of the participants in this study related their concern over the academic apathy among students. Eight of the participants referred to their students' indifference to educational success as a challenge. This number includes four out of the twelve affinitive educators and four of the nine facilitative educators. A South Dakota teacher simply remarked, "I would say motivation and apathy are the biggest [challenges] we combat with our kids. We have a problem in class with sleeping. Just plain don't want to do anything, head down, don't care." Another South Dakota high school teacher outlined just how extreme the apathy has become in some of her students: "Some of them I haven't even seen yet and this is how many weeks into the school? Or I've seen them maybe once every other week. I don't see a lot of my students on a regular basis."

A Montana educator offered an explanation for the academic apathy he regularly encounters. For him, student indifference results from a lack of self-confidence:

> Sometimes we try to fight through the stereotypes. . . . What I have found is they lack that confidence that they are good. They believe that they are not as skilled or not as smart. Even when I tell them they are, tell them until I'm blue in the face when I can see it and recognize it. But they don't want to let that go. Sometimes we've talked about that it is possibly a fear of failure. That if I don't try, I really didn't fail. But if I give everything that I've got and I fail, then I'm a failure, my family is a failure, and those types of things.

Another Montana teacher attributed the academic apathy he sees in students to the indifference of parents. This educator made the connection between lack of family support for education and student academic apathy: "But as far as education goes, I think a lot of these kids are struggling because they have no push from the home. Their parents don't care about education. Consequently, it reflects on their kids. They don't care either. 'I'm just here because I have to be here.'"

One South Dakota teacher regarded academic apathy as symptomatic of greater problematic personal and social issues. As a result, teachers must exercise diligence and patience with their students:

> A lot of these kids come here thinking they can't succeed, that they are dumb, they can't read, or they can't pass a class because they have that label on them. To get them in there and see some success and to start to really have confidence with themselves is what I love about my kids because you see a different child. I mean, you just see a totally different child when they start to see success within themselves. They are no longer hiding under their hoodie, their head is not down. They are showing some pride in themselves and their work, they ask questions. Sometimes it takes a lot to get there. But for me that is very rewarding. . . . These kids are not looking for that [academic success] because most of the time they don't want the work. They don't care what their grade is. They are here because it's a safe place. It's better here than it is at home. . . . So they are looking for basic needs when they come here. . . . Education is usually at the bottom of the list. It's, "Oh, this is what I have to do to get my basic needs met."

Student suicides represent the most heart-wrenching challenge facing the participants. Sadly, as educators they see this tragedy all too frequently. Eight of the respondents (four affinitive educators and four facilitative educators) specifically discussed the suicides of their students. The interviews reveal the pain resulting from these tragic events. A Montana teacher fighting through her tears quietly offered, "The biggest challenge we've had in the past year is our suicides. And one of those that happened in the spring was one of my kids in here. I'm not over it yet. None of us are, I think, in this school. We're walking wounded. You can't deal with it. It's like, why?"

A number of the educators found that the emotional burden resulting from student suicides was almost too great to bear. One Montana educator mournfully reflected, "You know, the last couple of months have been pretty tough, the last couple of years really. We've had kids who have been committing suicide. . . . It's too emotionally draining, something that [you don't know] unless you've took a call like that or dealt with that and then reconnected to the community knowing these kids when they were little kids. If I would have known that those kinds of things were going to happen I don't think I would have ever gotten into the business because those things are extremely difficult to deal with."

A South Dakota teacher outlined just how extreme the situation is for reservation children. The extent of student suicides in her teaching career is incomprehensible. It is also difficult to imagine the pain this educator, and others like her, endure:

> I think we lose out on where they are coming from and how hard their lives are. I think I don't know it all the time because every year, every year, we lose at least one kid to suicide. So in thirteen years I have lost thirteen kids. And those are just the ones I know about. And that's in addition to car accidents or whatnot. I don't think things on the reservations are being properly addressed as far as how dire of a situation it is for our kids. We think it is bad but I don't think we have any idea. . . . I am sure a lot of it has to do with drugs and alcohol but I think it's more of an abandonment issue with our kids. . . . They are alone and that breaks my heart because they come here and there is no reason why they should be alone here. . . . This should be the safe haven.

All educators, at least on some level, must deal with the problems associated with their students. Most students do not check their behavioral problems, poor attitudes, or emotional turmoil at the door of the school. And the reasons behind their troubles are complex. There are many sources of the problems displayed by students. Some issues result from personal and emotional problems, and others derive from perplexing social conditions. No doubt most problematic issues associated with students, whether disciplinary problems, academic apathy, or student suicide, are due to a combination of both personal and social difficulties. The intricate origin, nature, and consequences of student issues create a lot of confusion, frustration, and even anguish among educators. As a result, how educators interpret and respond to student issues can vary a great deal.

It is revealing that affinitive educators did not appear to be as concerned with disciplinary problems as did facilitative educators. It is unlikely that affinitive educators have fewer occurrences of misbehavior in their classrooms than facilitative educators, yet most of them never mentioned discipline as a challenge. On the other hand, virtually all of the facilitative educators refer to discipline as a challenge. It is possible that affinitive educators, given their predisposition to build relationships with students, are more likely to exercise greater tolerance of student disruptions. Several affinitive educators told me that giving students greater latitude in their conduct was part of their strategy in establishing personal connections. For instance, one South Dakota elementary teacher explained, "There's more to it than just sitting down and being quiet. I think that sometimes some of the teachers don't like it because I was more relaxed. If the kids were talking, it didn't bother me. They didn't have to be quiet and paying attention and just doing that. . . . They trusted who I was."

Conversely, facilitative educators regarded student misconduct as an impediment to effective instruction. From their point of view, discipline issues represent a challenge to performing their most important role—serving as an effective educator. The point is, however, that student discipline (while most certainly connected to larger social issues) is essentially a classroom management concern. In other words, it is something that educators have some control over. Unlike facilitative educators, affinitive educators do not see discipline as a major concern to the way they conduct a classroom. For them, too much emphasis on classroom management may be as much of a problem as too little.

On the other hand, while student academic apathy and student suicide represent personal, emotional problems, they are also associated with broader conditions in the community. Therefore, educators have little control over conditions producing academic apathy and student suicide. Both types of educators recognized the challenges presented by the general lack of interest toward education in Native communities. Student academic apathy likely results in large measure from the persistent indifference on reservations toward education. Additionally, student suicide is connected to the social trauma found in Native communities. Native youth attempt suicide at levels unmatched by their peers (Willmon-Haque & BigFoot, 2008), American Indian children have higher suicide rates than any other racial or ethnic group in the United States (Mullany et al., 2009), and suicide is the second-leading cause of deaths among Native young people between the ages of fifteen and twenty-four, behind unintentional injuries and accidents (Pem, 2010).

Much more so than discipline problems, academic apathy and student suicide reflect serious conditions found on reservations. The participants told me that they could exercise more control over discipline problems than they could over academic apathy or student suicide. Largely because disciplinary issues confront the very way facilitative educators define their responsibilities, they were more inclined to see them as a challenge. However, there is no escaping the larger social problems producing both student academic apathy and student suicide. These issues impact educators no matter how they define their roles and the participants had no choice but to deal with these problems head-on. As a result, both affinitive educators and facilitative educators perceived these issues as challenges.

School Staff Issues

School staff issues, the fourth theoretical construct, include problems located within the school system. Fourteen of the twenty-one educators indicated difficulties arising from at least one of the dimensions included under this theoretical construct. Specifically, dimensions of school staff issues involve ineffective educators, disregard for American Indian educators, staff turnover, and prejudicial attitudes held by some non-Native teachers.

Ten of the participants discussed problems associated with ineffective educators. Not surprisingly, a larger proportion of facilitative educators (seven of the nine) mentioned this issue compared to affinitive educators (three of the twelve). Moreover, affinitive educators and facilitative educators focused on different attributes they regarded as ineffective. For instance, affinitive educators tended to protest the detachment from reservation communities among some non-Native educators. Specifically, they reported reluctance among some of their non-Native colleagues to participate in community or school activities. As a result, they believed these individuals were not as effective as they might be otherwise. A Montana teacher, an affinitive educator, noted her displeasure with those who demonstrate little investment in the school and community: "I also think that sometimes we have teachers here who don't even have any vested interest in our school and come here to collect a paycheck and leave. They don't really care and our students know it. And they wonder why we are not effective. And I know not everyone can live here, the housing is hard to find. But there's ways you can come and connect to these kids, like attend events or just be around."

The facilitative educators, on the other hand, related concerns over the professional competence of some of their fellow educators. One principal, a facilitative educator, expressed his apprehension about the teacher training received by some of the instructors in his school:

> We are kind of holding teachers' feet to the fire as far as lesson planning and being effective. But if I didn't do that and I let them do what they have done in the past, nothing is going to change here. . . . I think they need to be a little more strict as far as what they need to do. . . . The teachers we have in our building here we're having to reteach as far as effective strategies, classroom management is huge, those sorts of things. I think the big thing is there has to come a point where we have people coming in, administrators or teacher leaders, and realize that we have to do a better job as educators. We have to be effective in the classrooms. Research says that if you have good lesson plans and you know strategies and you're very strong in your content knowledge that a lot of the stuff we're dealing with on the reservations will take care of themselves as far as the educational system.

An even more alarming issue surrounds an indifference to the suffering of students. On occasion, the accounts related by the participants take on a deeply troubling nature. For instance, a Montana principal reflected,

> I think the longer I am in this business, and hopefully this gets shared with some people, there's a huge element of caring with these kids that if you come and you want to work on an Indian reservation school, and if you are going to [do] it because the benefits are good and the paycheck is decent and it's just a job, I would highly recommend that you don't because these kids need people in their lives who truly care about what they are doing. And I hate to use this example, but if a kid comes up to you and says, "My parents were drinking and I didn't have anything to eat last night and they were beating on each other," and you're the teacher who is listening to this, legally you pick up the phone and call that in. But I would suspect that some of our teachers don't. Because they don't care. They don't care that the kid hasn't eaten, they don't care that the kid's parents have been beating on each other. I mean, if you're going to want to come and work on a reservation school and you're willing to pick that phone up and

make that phone call because you really, really care about the kid, and when a parent comes storming in here pissed because you made that phone call, because that will happen. Those are the things that I think educators on reservation schools deal with and they really test your wherewithal. Do you really want to be here teaching? Because some days working in a school like this, teaching isn't primary. It's not. Listening to kids and just having conversations with kids sometimes takes precedence over long division.

Seven of the participants believed some people do not regard American Indian educators as highly as non-Native educators. Thus, the disregard for American Indian educators is the second dimension of school staff issues. Affinitive educators reported these perceptions more frequently than facilitative educators. Six of the twelve affinitive educators compared to only one of the nine facilitative educators related this perception.

The participants suggested that a lack of respect for the abilities of American Indian educators lies at the heart of this challenge. An educator in Montana explained, "It was hard for me because I had to prove myself to the non-Indian teachers, who kind of looked down their noses at me, thinking, 'Well, what kind of teacher is she going to be?'" Or as a South Dakota principal frankly stated, "I don't think that [a general disregard for the professional competence of American Indian educators] has fully changed. It has to a degree, but I don't think I get the full respect. There are very few of us Native administrators." A Montana teacher outlined her feelings about the disrespect she and other American Indian educators encounter: "Pretty much all the Indian teachers stick together. But in a way we have to work doubly hard to get any kind of respect because we are always generalized. People [non-Native educators] always say that we are too easy on the kids, which isn't true. We just do different things with them because we know the things they are doing aren't working so we're trying to do different things. I think that is one thing I always hear is that 'so-and-so is too lenient with the kids.'"

A Montana principal displayed his frustration during the interview. His remarks suggest the latent as well as overt racism that, in his view, permeates reservation school systems:

> The problem is there is a racial line in schools like ours. There really is, as much as you try to say there isn't, there really is. Because it's still dominated by this white, you know, educational system that says this needs to happen. So sometimes I think, I really feel that your Indian teachers and maybe administrators are looked at as a little—I won't use the word inferior, but in the rung of things here's your white teachers [one hand

raised above the other]. It always seems like they are just a little above the Indian. And people are going to say, "No, no, that's not it," but it is. That's the way it is and I think that whites, a lot of whites, come into a school like ours with this attitude of, "I'm better than you and I'm going to teach you people the way it should be." There's some people like that.

A few of the participants believed these kinds of attitudes are not isolated to the building level but also are found at the district level. For instance, another Montana principal vented his dissatisfaction with the lack of regard for Native educators by saying, "I have a feeling that our school board still believes that Native American administrators aren't as worthy as their counterparts that are non-Native. And it may be just one of those things that I have a feeling about. One of the things I do know is other administrators have come in here and are higher on the salary scale."

One-third of the participants expressed concern over the rapidity of staff turnover in their schools or on the reservation in general. Specifically, seven individuals, including four of the affinitive educators and three of the facilitative educators, related alarm over the staff attrition in their schools. They contended that meeting the challenges facing reservation schools requires the staying power of educators. A Montana high school teacher discussed her apprehension over the recent addition of several new teachers. Her school had endured a high rate of teacher turnover and was facing significant problems, including difficulties meeting adequate yearly progress (AYP) as mandated by NCLB:

> I'm hoping we will keep them but they are all first-year, young teachers. I can't honestly say that this is where they will want to spend their life. But I think if we can get everything else ironed out we are going to have to go with the people who are going to stay here. . . . That's what I feel is probably our biggest problem . . . [and] it's going to be a challenge to be here. You're going to have some struggles. But you're going to have opportunities to grow in different ways as an educator that you never thought you would have. Don't you think everyone should want a challenge in their career?

With dry humor, a South Dakota principal reflected on the perplexing history of turnover among her school's administrative leaders: "This is the first year ever we didn't have staff turnover—in administrator turnover. I'm certainly not the answer, but before they talked me out of coming out of the classroom we had five principals in two years. A couple of them just weren't administrators. They'd bring them from the outside [outside the reservation].

One was here for two weeks. He liked it. We thought he would be fine but his wife came and took a look and told him it was either his job or his family. So he moved back."

Condescending, arrogant, and outright racist attitudes displayed by non-Native educators alarmed some of the participants. Therefore, the prejudicial attitudes of some non-Native educators represent the fourth dimension of school staff issues. Seven of the educators (five affinitive educators and two facilitative educators) described prejudicial attitudes among some teachers as a challenge. A few accounts outlined blatant racism toward American Indian students and families. A Montana teacher related an episode that occurred at a school she had previously served. This particular school is located in a different community but on the same reservation as she is on in her current position. The account depicts the brazen bigotry of some teachers entrusted with the education of Native children:

> I remember we were at a staff meeting one time and we were told we had to go out and meet the families of our students, which I thought was a great idea and I was excited and everything. And our principal said, "You need to shake their hands and look them in the eye. Be very respectful. These are the parents of your students." And then one of the girls [a young teacher] made a comment, "Oh, are you going to give us diaper wipes for us to wipe our hands afterward?" We all just looked at her like, "I cannot believe you just said that!" I was just amazed that she would say something like that. And then one of the other teachers, he was one of the other Indian teachers too, he said, "You know we need to be really respectful. These are our children's parents. We need to be respectful."

A South Dakota teacher, too, voiced her concerns over the condescending attitudes of some non-Native colleagues. The racial prejudice evidenced by some teachers as related by this participant is quite disconcerting:

> Just because we are Native, we're poverty stricken or whatever you want to call it, some people say, "Well, they live in a Third World country." People who come from [two border towns near the reservation] say that. They come across the border and they say, "Oh, God, I'm in a Third World country again. I can't believe I'm down here!" And yet they take these [teaching] jobs. And they come down here with that attitude and try to teach our kids. And that's not going to work for them because they don't become part of our community. . . . We have so many labels that we listen to as a people we don't need people who come here and believe those. Instead, look at each individual, each child, in their eyes and say, "I see who you are. You are awesome. You can learn. You

can do this. I know you can." And seeing the strengths those little ones have, if they did that, our people would go so far.

Virtually all the challenges identified by the participants were related to larger social issues in the community. However, more than any other set of challenges, school staff issues relate to concerns within the school itself. Moreover, it is also on these challenges that affinitive educators and facilitative educators evidence the most noticeable differences in perceptions and experiences. Consider these patterns: facilitative educators more than affinitive educators regarded ineffective educators as a problem; affinitive educators more than facilitative educators believed Native educators do not receive the same level of respect as non-Native educators; and affinitive educators were much more likely than facilitative educators to point out the racist tendencies of some non-Native educators. Of the four dimensions of school staff issues, only on staff turnover do affinitive educators and facilitative educators appear to hold similar perceptions. I will discuss the difference in these perceptions in greater detail later in this chapter. For the moment, let me address the experience shared in common by affinitive educators and facilitative educators.

These two types of educators share a concern over staff turnover simply because it is a major, long-term problem in many reservation school systems (Erickson et al. 2008). Reservation school districts, like many high-poverty school districts, frequently represent convenient places for new teachers to begin their careers and subsequently move on (Hardy, 2005). Transitional staff is also much more likely to occur because many new teachers are non-Native and have no real ties to the community, as so many of the affinitive educators were quick to point out. The experiences of these educators reinforce the need for stable and committed school staff serving reservation students (Erickson et al., 2008).

COMPARISON OF AFFINITIVE EDUCATORS AND FACILITATIVE EDUCATORS

One of the fundamental issues driving this research is the relationship between the self-defined roles described by the educators and the major challenges they identified. To examine this relationship requires a comparison of affinitive educators and facilitative educators. I grouped the challenges identified by the participants under four theoretical constructs: reservation social conditions, attitudes toward education, student-related issues, and school staff issues. Generally, the two types of educators revealed more similarities than differences in the challenges they identified. Affinitive and facilitative educators held comparable views on the challenges presented by reservation social conditions. Moreover, they related relatively comparable perceptions on challenges arising from the attitudes toward education (affinitive educators were more likely to identify community scrutiny on Native educators) and most student-related issues (facilitative educators were more likely to express concern about discipline problems). The most notable differences surrounded their views on school staff issues. Facilitative educators demonstrated greater concern over ineffective educators, while affinitive educators were more likely to discuss problems related to a general disregard for Native educators and prejudicial attitudes held by some non-Native educators.

While affinitive educators and facilitative educators certainly evidence more areas of agreement than not, a close consideration of the differences between the two types of educators reveals some important patterns. Generally, the issues affinitive educators found disconcerting but the facilitative educators did not involve social perceptions and interpersonal relationships. These individuals discussed such concerns as community scrutiny on American Indian educators, disregard for Native educators, and racist attitudes among non-Native educators. Facilitative educators tended to identify challenges preventing schools from effectively educating children. They discussed problems arising from discipline problems and ineffective educators. Affinitive educators were not especially troubled by these issues.

It is my conclusion that the way the participants defined their roles subtly but significantly impacts the kinds of challenges they perceived. However, it is important to ask, What can account for *both* the similarities and the differences in perceptions on the challenges identified by these educators? In order to arrive at an explanation, it is useful to divide the challenges into two basic types: core challenges and peripheral challenges.

Core challenges are issues so large and perplexing they transcend concerns that may be specific to particular professional roles. In other words, core challenges place a heavy burden on educators no matter how they define their roles, and are so pervasive that neither affinitive educators nor facilitative educators could escape them. As a result, core challenges become part of the experience for all who serve reservation schools. This is the reason why affinitive educators and facilitative educators identified them with relatively comparable frequency. Eight of the challenges identified by the participants constitute core challenges: poverty, family dysfunctions, alcohol and drug abuse, community indifference, lack of family support, academic apathy, student suicides, and staff turnover.

Peripheral challenges include issues that, although perplexing compared to core challenges, are not as insidious and are more idiosyncratic to the way the educators defined their roles. Affinitive educators were more likely than facilitative educators to describe problems such as community scrutiny on American Indian educators, disregard for American Indian educators, and prejudicial attitudes among some teachers. These are all associated with affinitive educators' emphasis on interpersonal relations and the importance of serving as a role model. Conversely, peripheral challenges for facilitative educators included problems arising from ineffective educators and classroom disruptions. These concerns connect with the way facilitative educators defined their role as educators. They contended the most important role for an educator is to be as effective as possible in order to ensure he or she provides students with quality instruction and learning experiences. Therefore, peripheral challenges include issues facilitative educators believed prevent schools from performing those duties fully and efficiently.

CONCLUSION

I found the challenges the participants described to be both important and insightful, but I was also a little surprised by what they did not say in the interviews. Previous researchers have found teachers most commonly identify time restrictions, unsupportive administration, lack of autonomy, poor work environment, low student performance, and low salaries among their most serious challenges (Brunetti, 2001; Cockburn, 2000; Darling-Hammond, 2003; Pearson & Moomaw, 2005; Perrachione, Rosser, & Petersen, 2008; Tickle, Chang, & Kim, 2011). While some of the educators did mention many of these challenges either directly or indirectly, they did not indicate they were of foremost concern. Generally, the issues typically reported in the literature are internal to the educational institution itself. The participants in this study tended to describe challenges largely associated with serious social and personal problems resulting outside the school. Nevertheless, these issues heavily influence their experiences as educators. In particular, the core challenges are of this nature. On the other hand, except for community scrutiny on American Indian educators, the peripheral challenges relate to internal conditions within the school system.

The literature provides scant insight on the experiences of American Indian educators in general and virtually no insight on the challenges they experience. What little research does exist tends to center on the issue of community and parent relations (Coladarci, 1983; Robinson-Zanartu & Majel-Dixon, 1996; Wilkinson, 2005). For instance, Erickson and colleagues (2008) found community support was one of the most important factors related to job satisfaction for those who teach American Indian children. While their research included both American Indian and non-Native teachers, it does relate to the findings in this research regarding the participants' frustrations with community indifference to education and lack of family support for education.

Other researchers, too, have reported on the prevalence of community indifference toward education on reservations. Notable in this regard are the findings reported by Alan Peshkin (1997) from his ethnographic research on a tribally controlled boarding school in New Mexico. Despite the fact that American Indian educators primarily staffed the school and it enjoyed cultural and educational autonomy in its operation, when compared to other New Mexico high school students its pupils scored lower on ACT tests and exhibited higher levels of attrition. Peshkin concludes the members of the Pueblo communities served by the school deem it a culturally foreign institution and thus manifest indifferent attitudes about its mission.

The challenges facing the participants in this study are numerous and complex. They require much from the educators. But there is also another side of their experience: challenges typically bring rewards. Just as the educators spoke with candor about the difficulties they face on a daily basis, they were just as open regarding the rewards serving reservation children and communities. The next chapter examines the proverbial "other side of the coin."

CHAPTER 4

If I Made a Difference for One
Intrinsic Rewards Serving Reservation Students

> *I have a cousin that's visiting from California and the night before last she asked me, "Do you think you will always stay here? Do you think you will always be here?" And I said, "Well, yeah. I think I will." And she goes, "Why? There's nothing here! You could do so much!" And I said, "But I am doing so much! This is where I choose to live and I think that I've hit some kids' hearts. And if I made a difference for one, that is worth it all."*
> —Montana middle school teacher reflecting on her life and profession

I got to the school just as dawn was beginning to break. Not sure exactly where the school was located deep in the reservation, I made sure to be early in case I needed to search the numerous back roads in order to be on time. I caught a glimpse of a school bus in the distance, and allowed it to guide me to the school. Traveling over the twisting, paved roads with the haunting silhouette of the landscape around, I mentally reviewed the interview guide questions while also pondering what I had learned in previous interviews. I was about to learn a lot more. Upon later reflection, driving through the disappearing darkness seemed like a metaphor for the day's coming events. I was nearing greater enlightenment. The lesson for this day would be about the uniquely powerful intrinsic rewards gained from serving one's people.

The last two days had not gone well for him. As we sat in the empty, dimly lit classroom before the school day began, the teacher took a long drink of coffee and leaned back in his chair. He was a big man who served not only as a teacher, but also as the high school football coach. He looked every bit the part and I thought he could be straight out of central casting. The day before, an intoxicated student had backed his car into this teacher's car, doing considerable damage. The student did not have insurance and his parents were unable to pay for the repairs. He was understandably angry, and yet his concern for the student never wavered. Indeed, he used the occasion to evaluate his role as an educator and his responsibilities according to the traditions of his tribe. Although too humble to tell me so, I later learned he is recognized as a spiritual leader and an emerging elder. For him, leading and teaching younger people through personal example go hand in hand with traditional beliefs. Even adversities, small and large, offer occasion to teach, learn, and serve. These moments also provide inestimable rewards for those who understand their significance:

> Yesterday that kid who hit my car, he was inebriated when he got here. Pulled in, backed up, boom, hit my car. I was angry at first but then you think about it. That family that kid comes from, they don't have nothing. He don't have insurance. And if the school don't pay for it, I will have to get it fixed myself. But that's one of the preachings. . . . I reflect back and wonder, Is there anything I could have done different? Is there anything I could have done a little bit better? Is there somebody I forgot or somebody I missed who I could have helped? . . . Our preachings say that when you help children learn, any which way, it don't manner if you teach them how to fix a bike. When you are helping children, your rewards come from the Creator. So I have always followed that rule. You know, getting a paycheck is great, too. It helps pay the bills. But the rewards that come from the Creator benefit your children as well as your family.

FRUIT OF A DAY'S WORK

Historian Jacques Barzun once remarked, "In teaching you cannot see the fruit of a day's work. It is invisible and remains so, maybe for twenty years." The educators in this study faced a myriad of challenges, but they also gained enormous rewards from their service. Yet, as Barzun suggests, they understood many of those rewards must be deferred. I have the feeling that for most of the educators I met, it did not matter that they may not see the fruit of their efforts for another twenty years—if they personally see them at all. These individuals truly believed they are contributing to the survival of their people. This belief motivated them and kept them going. As one South Dakota teacher who compared the challenges to the rewards explained, "I think it is sometimes easier to focus on the challenges but it's the rewards that keep you teaching. The rewards stay with me a lot longer than the challenges do." Or, as a Montana teacher related, "These are our kids. We're all related somehow. . . . They are all our kids, so we just have to work harder and find new ways and keep trying. . . . The rewards outweigh anything."

The educators had reason to remain optimistic, for indeed they directly and significantly contribute to the survival of their people—if only one child at a time. They seemed to viscerally understand their efforts have a lasting, enduring quality, and that what they are doing will not only forever change the lives of some children, but also change the reservation itself. A South Dakota principal simply and succinctly exemplified the copious optimism for the future by concluding our interview with saying, "I just feel that I was put in the right place and I've been doing the best I can. And I think I really have made some difference."

This chapter examines the intrinsic rewards described by the participants. Unfortunately, the educators had less to say about rewards than they did about the challenges. However, the greater the challenges, the more significant the rewards. The participants revealed five different intrinsic rewards: witnessing the success of their students, receiving the appreciation expressed by others, understanding they make a difference in students' lives, being aware that they are helping the reservation, and recognizing that they assist in tribal cultural preservation. I group these rewards into two basic types: affirming rewards and altruistic rewards. This chapter compares the two types of educators with the kinds of rewards they described and outlines some subtle differences in their experiences.

Affirming Rewards

Affirming rewards serve to confirm and validate the participants' efforts. Analysis of the interviews indicates two dimensions of this theoretical construct: witnessing the success of students and receiving the appreciation and respect offered by others. By all appearances, affirming rewards are very important to the educators in this sample. Twenty of the twenty-one participants mentioned at least one of the two dimensions of affirming rewards during the interviews.

Understandably, the participants took great delight in the accomplishments of their students. They found that personal contributions to students' achievements served to affirm their work. Sixteen of the twenty-one educators referred to witnessing the success of their students as an intrinsic reward. Given their propensity to emphasize the instrumental benefits of academic achievement, one might expect facilitative educators would be more inclined to identify this theme as a reward. However, this did not appear to be the case at all. Affinitive educators and facilitative educators displayed virtually identical perceptions about the success of students. Nine of the twelve affinitive educators and seven of the nine facilitative educators alluded to witnessing the achievements of students as an important intrinsic reward.

For a few of the educators, the rewards gained from observing the success of their students had immediate payoffs. These individuals noted the big and small achievements of students and were buoyed by their success. A Montana principal related the sense of triumph he felt in seeing former students return to the reservation as teachers: "But the intrinsic part, sometimes [are] the successes you see. I got a couple of former students who are coming back to teach now. And have chosen to come back. They didn't have to. . . . The one that I'm thinking of right now, he came back and actually said that he is a teacher because I was his teacher. And he is coming back here so that he could help out some of the kids the same way that I did. I mean, to hear that said is a big motivator."

Others described everyday successes as extremely valuable to their morale. A South Dakota elementary teacher related the joy she experiences with each small accomplishment of her students:

> I just wanted to bring our people up, bring these little kids up. And just by getting in a classroom and letting these kids explore and not just directing all the time but showing them what they can do with themselves. In my first year of teaching, I had students who were reading at two grade levels higher by the time they left. They just took off. I didn't hold them back. I didn't tell them, "Oh, you're poverty stricken. You can't learn." That word [poverty] just gets to me every time! . . . It's still the same. I just get that feeling every time I see one of my little ones say, "That's a letter M. It makes an Mmm sound!" And I go, "Yes!" I just love it. It just boosts me every day. I go, "Oh my God, this is awesome!" I love it. This is my job. I just love it.

Frequently they mentioned the satisfaction of seeing students graduate from high school. Even elementary teachers often attend high school graduations in order to personally share with their former students' academic successes. A Montana elementary teacher related, "I like it that I see people graduating and going on, and going to college, going for their heart's desire, whatever type of job they would like to have. That really makes it. I like that. And I've seen umpteen kids go through school and now I have their kids in school."

One South Dakota elementary principal described the extraordinary lengths she goes to in order to celebrate the successes of her former students. On occasion, she must travel hundreds of miles in order to attend their high school graduations. She regarded participation in events celebrating the accomplishments of students as part of the responsibilities as a tribal leader. She explained, "The students' successes. I try, and I miss some of them, I try to go to every one of their high school graduations. An example is [name of a boarding school] this year. They had a pretty big class. I don't know, there were seventy or so, and two of them were my former students."

A number of the educators spoke of the deferred nature of the intrinsic rewards serving Native children and communities. They understood the seeds they sow will take years to germinate and bloom. A South Dakota educator mused, "Well, I guess when I see my students that I've had years ago and I see them and they're doing really well I feel like I had a part of that. Maybe a small part. And I feel like this is where I am supposed to be, this is actually where I am supposed to be."

Indeed, the deferred nature of intrinsic rewards proved to be a common sentiment. A Montana principal described what she would like to see as her final achievement as an educator: "I would like my legacy to be—the last class I taught, they were third graders—to have every one of them graduate from high school and go to college. That would be awesome, totally awesome. And then I could say, 'I was their third grade teacher, and I knew every one of them could make it.'"

A South Dakota teacher philosophically reflected on the nature of her contribution as an educator. As she considered the future, she concluded her ultimate and greatest reward will result from the achievements of her students. With great contemplation, she asked, "How would I mark what I have done? I could do a lot of things. I could write books. But I think what would really, really encourage me or let me know that I am doing something is when my first-year class graduates. When they are seniors, I think that will empower everything I am doing."

The appreciation expressed by others affirmed the contributions made by the educators and served as another important intrinsic reward. Almost half of the participants (ten of the twenty-one) alluded to the importance of the gratitude offered by others. However, the analysis of the interviews revealed a difference between the two types of educators. The affinitive educators were more likely to refer to the importance of this reward than were the facilitative educators. In fact, whereas seven of the twelve affinitive educators discussed how important it is to receive the appreciation from others, only three of the nine facilitative educators described this reward.

Most of the educators recounted simple, mundane, but genuine gestures of gratitude, expressions of appreciation that carried a great deal of meaning and had significant consequences on the morale of the participants. A South Dakota elementary teacher discussed the importance of the gratitude shown by her young students: "Whenever it really gets bad, it's always the adults. And I think, 'Gosh, I should quit and go do something else.' But a child will come up to me and give me a hug and that's the end of that, I'm back! Forget the adults. They can do whatever they want to do. I'm here for the kids."

These ordinary events in which people voluntarily offered simple expressions of appreciation and respect reinforced their sense of purpose and served to fortify their efforts. A Montana educator related the following story:

> I walk into the grocery store and here comes a kid up to me and I haven't taught this kid for maybe fifteen years and he was probably one of the toughest kids I ever had to teach. I've taught K through 12, and that kid gave me fits but I never gave up on him. And now that guy wants to come up to me and says, "You know, I made something out of myself. I want to thank you. I enjoyed your class." . . . Those are the kinds of things that's really worth a paycheck right there. When somebody comes up and says, "Thanks, I liked when you talked about Indians." I taught Indian studies. "I liked when you did that." It personalized it for that student. Those kinds of things. That's what makes it.

Occasionally the participants related tender accounts of the small, sincere gestures made by students. What may appear as a fleeting moment in a person's career frequently held special significance and resonated many years afterward. A South Dakota principal shared such an experience that had occurred many years previously:

> When you work in tribal schools there's a lot of dysfunctional behavior. I remember one year having a handful of boys who were just naughty. But I knew where they were coming from because I had lived in [name of reservation community] all these years and knew their families and I knew it was because of dysfunctional behavior. And I remember one little boy who I struggled with all year. And I remember fighting for him. His parents didn't care. He had a mother, no father, was not being taken care of, and we set up meetings to try to get him some help so he would be safe. And he was placed out of the home. And I remember at the end of the year, there was nobody in the classroom, and he comes walking in with the man who ran the home he was living in, and he brought me a bouquet of flowers. [Tears well up from the memory.] Those are the things that drove me.

Unfortunately, these kinds of intrinsic rewards could also be double-edged. At times, such expressions of appreciation came with reminders of lost opportunities. One South Dakota teacher explained that occasionally she must console those who too late come to realize the value of her guidance:

They remember. Things that you wouldn't even think somebody would remember. But I have a lot of that. I mean, that's a pat on the back for me. To have someone come over and say, "This is my grandchild or this is my child and this person really inspired me to do the best I can." And even the sad times. I've had kids call me from prison and say "Miss [participant's name], I didn't listen and look at where I'm at. I sure wish I would have paid more attention and did what you told me to do. And now I'm here and nobody cares."

While most of the participants described personal and informal expressions of gratitude offered by other people, a few did identify more formal and community-based displays of recognition and appreciation. The account shared by a South Dakota principal underscores the cultural significance when the community acts to express its gratitude for the service rendered by an educator:

We had our annual wacipi [powwow] and we honored a person that was retiring. So we got all that done and I came back over to the office to get some honorarium checks to give out. And I got back to the gym and there was a chair with a star quilt on it in the middle. And they said, "Miss [name of participant], would you please come up to the center?" And the staff honored me. And one of the honors they gave me was an Indian name. And the name they gave me is, "Helps the People Woman." And then, after that I look and I see my family in the corner and they kept it a secret for who knows how long. And I was very humbled.

Whether it was observing the success of students or receiving expressions of appreciation, affirming rewards appear to carry a special kind of significance for the educators. Certainly, their accounts revealed how they gained strength, vitality, and pride from these kinds of reinforcements. Likely because they perceive a great deal of community indifference toward education, the participants also readily embraced the renewing power of affirmation. A Montana teacher simply but enthusiastically exclaimed, "I feel I have a purpose. It motivates me. People in the community have complimented me and want their kids in my classroom because they understand what I am trying to do with these kids!"

The affinitive educators in particular were inclined to discuss the importance of affirming rewards in their experience as educators. However, it would be a great mistake to interpret this to mean that affinitive educators were somehow less confident (or worse, more superficial) than facilitative educators and, thus, required more confirmation of their work. It must be remembered that affinitive educators were more likely to come from culturally traditional backgrounds than were the facilitative educators. Perhaps because the affinitive educators came from strong communal backgrounds where the affirmation from others is an important part of the culture, they simply were more likely to identify affirming rewards as significant. One thing is clear: the intrinsic rewards derived from actually seeing students' successes and gaining the appreciation of others was manifestly important to the participants.

Altruistic Rewards

The educators frequently indicated they gain gratification from the knowledge that their efforts serve others. Three themes comprise the dimensions of a theoretical construct I call altruistic rewards: understanding they make a difference in students' lives, contributing to the betterment of the reservation, and assisting to preserve tribal culture. Seventeen of the twenty-one educators described deriving rewards from at least one of the dimensions of altruistic rewards.

Given the demands of the profession combined with the generally low pay relative to the academic training and social responsibility attached to it, the education profession historically has attracted dedicated individuals devoted to service. Virtually all educators first and foremost serve for the good of children. Sixteen of the twenty-one participants described the rewards derived from the knowledge they make a difference in the lives of children. Eight of the twelve affinitive educators and eight of the nine facilitative educators specifically referred to the awareness that they make a difference for students as an important intrinsic reward.

Frequently, the rewards the participants described have a special significance. They faced enormous difficulties and the severity of the social problems found on the reservation enhances the satisfaction gained from impacting a child's life. A South Dakota high school teacher understood her influence may be all that stands between success and tragedy for many of her students:

> It's rewarding to not only see them succeed but be happy, and see them grow as kids. But at the same time to feel that you are making a difference in their life as far as you are the one they come to when there's problems. And they are reaching out to someone when they have the red flags that something is going on versus doing the other things we know they do which is fight, smoke, drink, cut, huff. You know that they are finding an outlet that's a personal relationship and not the other kinds of things.

Rather than pointing out specific examples of how they have impacted a student, a number of the participants described this intrinsic reward in abstract terms. Nevertheless, they derived a sense of accomplishment from the intuitive understanding they positively influence children. For example, a South Dakota educator reflected, "It's always a good feeling to know that you are making a difference in reservation children's lives. That has always been my reward if I can improve a student's or a child's life. That was one of my goals as a professional and I try to impress upon them that education is important. In today's society, you can't hardly do anything without a decent education. So intrinsically it was trying to improve their lives as much as possible and go on and be a contributing member of society." A Montana teacher expressed similar experiences. He explained, "I'm trying to help these kids develop a sense of purpose and goals, something else than what they just have here. 'It's a big world out there.' I tell them. 'There's opportunity to go all over the place.' . . . The intrinsic reward is, I guess, the hope that those kids can find that opportunity."

The simple knowledge that they had changed a perception, altered an expectation, and expanded an ambition produced great rewards for the many of the educators and fueled their desire to continue with their service. As a South Dakota principal explained the rewards she gains from serving as an educator, "To leave an impression. I remember a little girl saying to me, 'When I grow up I want to be a principal,' knowing that now Native Americans can become principals and they can become teachers. So it's those kinds of things that have driven me to continue doing what I am doing."

While their efforts may not be evident for many years in the future, the participants recognized they are directly contributing to the betterment of the reservation. They were both educators as well as instruments of community development. Ten of the twenty-one participants, nearly half, specifically discussed the intrinsic reward of knowing they are contributing to the improvement of the reservation. Four of the affinitive and six of the facilitative educators referred to this reward during the interviews. These individuals found great fulfillment in the awareness their efforts will eventually work to enhance the quality of life for the greater community. As one South Dakota educator described her feelings about the rewards she experiences, "Just being able to give back. I mean this is my community. To help kids succeed. And I know everybody. If I'm not related to them, I've taught their families, went to school with the grandparents. And it really helps me because I know everyone. I know where everyone lives."

A Montana educator framed the rewards of serving the community within the legacy he hopes to leave behind. This teacher obviously accepted the deferred nature of intrinsic rewards associated with assisting the community: "I feel good about what I do. I do my best for these kids and that's all I can do. I'm frustrated a lot of days. It's a frustrating process. But you get your moments. . . . I would hope that at some point I've motivated and inspired a few people. Whether that will happen or not remains to be seen. But I want to be thought of as somebody that cared about these kids and cared about education and recognized that education has positive benefits for our tribe and our community."

Another Montana teacher spoke of a desire to achieve specific accomplishments. For this educator, the potential benefits to the reservation are a natural, albeit hard-earned, part of being a Native educator:

> I think another reward is to be able to see students grow and learn. And I think what really makes my heart tickle is when kids can say, "You know Miss [participant's name], when I grow up I want to be a teacher like you." I don't know what it is, but that's what blesses me! And to see that I'm investing in our future. I think that our children are our future and I believe that somewhere down the road I've helped in the life of our next tribal chairman or tribal chairwoman, another doctor, or lawyer. So those are the rewards that I look at.

A powerful reward for a number of the participants was the awareness their efforts help to preserve tribal traditions and language. While fifteen of the twenty-one participants discussed the use of schools in the effort to preserve tribal culture (a topic addressed in more detail in chapter 7), eight individuals specifically described this contribution as an intrinsic reward. This number includes five of the twelve affinitive educators and two of the nine facilitative educators.

Those who identified the rewards gained from helping to preserve tribal culture either taught Native language subjects or are themselves speakers of the tribal language. Understandably, these individuals gained a tremendous sense of accomplishment from this reward. For example, a South Dakota tribal language and culture teacher exclaimed,

> It's awesome! It's really an awesome feeling being Native and being with our people based on our history and everything we couldn't do at one time and the things we can do today. That's the reward of it. But the rewards of knowing that you can be at home here and the children can come to school and can share what a beautiful heritage that

we have and where we come from. And to look at history in a different way rather than always looking at it as, "Oh, that was a terrible way. They were bad. How could they have done this to us?" Rather than look at it that way we can say, "This is what happened in our history and what is it that we are going to do to make a difference together today?"

A Montana tribal language teacher described the rewards gained from influencing young students. This individual took particular satisfaction in one of his former students who has proceeded to make a significant contribution to help preserve the tribal language:

> The reward is when you see kids in the hallway and they greet you in [the tribal language]. . . . And some of the older students that I've taught that are now adults, they come up to me and say, you know, they talk [the tribal language] and all. They say they got their start learning the language from my classroom. I think that is the reward right there. As long as you are promoting your language and enhancing your language development with the young ones and passing all your knowledge along. . . . There was a young gentleman who came through my door one time. I've had him since he was in sixth grade, seventh grade. Seen him grow up. And his family and his grandparents are really strong, traditional people. And he said, "I want to be like you one day." You know, I thought that was pretty good. He went to Missoula, got his degree, and now he is teaching at [the tribal college] here. And he is teaching the language.

Altruistic rewards originate within the person. Ultimately, few rewards may be more powerful than the visceral awareness that one makes a contribution. Standing on this conviction, the participants weathered many of the challenges they routinely faced. But there are some interesting differences between affinitive educators and facilitative educators.

Facilitative educators were somewhat more likely to describe altruistic rewards compared to affinitive educators. However, there is a complexity within this pattern of perceptions. The participants described three specific types of altruistic rewards: making a difference in students' lives, the awareness they help the reservation, and the satisfaction in working to preserve tribal culture. The affinitive educators identified only one altruistic reward (knowledge that they are assisting to preserve tribal culture) more frequently than the facilitative educators. Because more of the affinitive educators came from traditional backgrounds, such a disposition is not especially surprising. Half of the affinitive educators indicated they had some fluency in a tribal language and greater exposure to traditional culture. Likely they feel they can make greater contributions to cultural preservation compared to the less culturally oriented facilitative educators.

Facilitative educators were slightly more likely to describe the rewards gained from an understanding they make a difference in the lives of children (all but one of the facilitative educators mentioned this reward) and in the awareness they help the larger reservation community. Rewards such as these are the kinds of accomplishments an educator who highly esteems his or her professional competence would be inclined to cherish.

There is, of course, another explanation: altruistic rewards are likely the most common kind of intrinsic rewards experienced by educators all over the country (Cookson, 2005). Unfortunately for some, they may be the only intrinsic rewards.

COMPARISON OF AFFINITIVE EDUCATORS AND FACILITATIVE EDUCATORS

Affinitive educators and facilitative educators shared a number of significant intrinsic rewards. Most clearly, these types of educators found it gratifying to observe the success of their students (an affirming reward) and derived satisfaction from the knowledge they are making a difference in students' lives (an altruistic reward). Indeed, these two intrinsic rewards rate as the most common forms of gratification identified by both types of educators.

However, a closer examination of the interviews does reveal a few differences in the kinds of rewards affinitive educators and facilitative educators reported as most compelling. While I need to be careful not to make more of these differences than they merit, the data do suggest affinitive educators placed slightly greater emphasis on affirming rewards (which are externally derived), whereas facilitative educators were somewhat more likely to stress altruistic rewards (which are internally derived). For instance, the majority of affinitive educators identified both dimensions of affirming rewards as important to them. Among the twelve affinitive educators, nine regarded witnessing the success of students and seven identified receiving appreciation from others as important intrinsic rewards. On the other hand, the majority of facilitative educators only mentioned observing the success of students (seven of the nine) as a reward but not gaining the respect and appreciation from others (only three of the nine). In regard to altruistic rewards, the reverse pattern exists. Whereas the majority of facilitative educators described two of the altruistic rewards as important, the majority of affinitive educators mentioned only one of the themes. Specifically, among the nine facilitative educators, eight identified the awareness they make a difference in students' lives and six discussed helping to improve the reservation as intrinsic rewards. Conversely, the majority of affinitive educators (eight of the twelve) mentioned only making a difference in students' lives as an important intrinsic reward.

Does that mean affinitive educators value affirmative rewards more than altruistic rewards, and facilitative educators place greater value on altruistic rewards over affirming rewards? Such a claim would be ludicrous. If nothing else, there are hardly enough data to support such a position. Rather, these data suggest something else. Likely, the two types of educators experience similar rewards and esteem them in comparable fashion. Simply put, I seriously doubt there is any substantial difference in the intrinsic rewards these American Indian educators value. However, I do think the two types of educators are more sensitive to certain types of rewards merely as a result of the way they interpret their respective roles. Affinitive educators likely do not receive personal compliments at any greater rate than the facilitative educators, but those rewards stood out in their minds because they saw themselves as role models and work hard to build personal relationships. Personal feedback is critical when building interpersonal relationships and such rewards strengthen the role affinitive educators deem important. On the other hand, facilitative educators viewed their fundamental role as being competent educators who promote the benefits of education. These educators highly esteemed the potential contributions they make to the betterment of the reservation. That does not mean they make more valuable contributions toward community development than the affinitive educators, but it could mean these individuals were more prone to describe these kinds of rewards because they are consistent with and reinforce the role they perceived for themselves as educators.

CONCLUSION

Lieberman and Miller (1992) make an interesting observation regarding the intrinsic rewards associated with teaching. They suggest the most meaningful rewards come from students. Teachers frequently toil in cloistered settings. As a result, they often lack affirmation from their peers, thus students frequently become one of their most important sources of confirmation and validation:

> The greatest satisfaction for a teacher is the feeling of being rewarded by one's students. In fact, most of the time the students are the only source of rewards for most teachers. Isolated in their own classrooms, teachers receive feedback for their efforts from

the words, expressions, behaviors, and suggestions of the students. By doing well on a test, sharing a confidence, performing a task, indicating an interest, and reporting the effects of a teacher's influence, students let teachers know that they are doing a good job and are appreciated. Unlike other professionals who look to colleagues and supervisors for such feedback, teachers can only turn to children. (Lieberman & Miller, 1992, p. 2)

This observation partially applies to the educators in this study. They frequently discussed the rewards gleaned from witnessing the successes as well as receiving the appreciation expressed by their students. Indeed, children are the most important source of the intrinsic rewards they experience. However, the educators in this study also generally described deep connections to their communities. The reservations I visited are populated by people of profound communal bonds. Indeed, the notion of community surfaced when the participants talked about the roles they perform, the challenges they face, and, yes, about the rewards they gain. Pavel and colleagues (2002) describe an American Indian and Alaska Native teacher preparation program partnered between Northwest Indian College and Washington State University. Although they did not report on the intrinsic rewards derived from serving reservation communities, it is evident the students who participated in the program were motivated by a call of service to their people. Just as important, they also anticipated the challenges before them as educators in Native schools. Significantly, the students and faculty involved in the program recognized and embraced the unique community-oriented responsibilities of Native teachers serving American Indian and Alaska Native schools. Simply put, to serve as a Native educator in reservation schools is to truly serve the entire community.

Other researchers, too, have documented the significance of intrinsic rewards in recruiting and retaining teachers in rural schools. While these studies did not include reservation schools, the similarities with the experiences of the participants in this study are clear enough. For instance, researchers have found rural teachers highly regard such powerful intrinsic rewards as helping rural communities, predilection for a rural lifestyle, and preference for small, safe school environments (Ballou & Podgarsky, 1995; Johnson & Strange, 2007; Monk, 2007; Smith-Davis, 2002; Zost, 2010). These similarities notwithstanding, the intrinsic rewards described by the participants in my research also have a unique, almost paradoxical character. Their rewards were privately experienced, yet frequently community derived and shared. I am reminded of the South Dakota principal mentioned in this chapter. It was altogether fitting for the community to honor her with the tribal name "Helps the People Woman." When the educators in this study assist their students, they are doing nothing less than fulfilling ancient, traditional responsibilities. The rewards were highly personal and private, but they were also public, cultural expectations. This is perhaps one of the reasons why affinitive educators, who were more likely to be traditionally oriented, displayed greater sensitivity to the public attention on Native educators. They understood all too well their efforts directly contribute to the survival of their people, and the tribe expects this of them.

Every profession has those who do little more than work for a paycheck. For such individuals, intrinsic rewards are minimal, whereas the extrinsic rewards are virtually everything. Certainly, education as a profession is no different in that regard from other professional fields, yet it is safe to say that most educators who remain in the profession highly prize the intrinsic rewards derived from their service. And, to be fair, I assume many of the rewards identified by the participants of this research do not greatly differ from the intrinsic rewards valued by educators everywhere. As Peter Cookson reminds us,

> Very often in our culture, people don't think of their work as a calling. For many people, their work is a means to an end. They work for a paycheck in order to live their lives. But those of us who are called to teach have a true vocation. Our mission is to increase the world's capacity for growth by enabling each of our students to fully maximize his or her talents, imagination, analytical skills, and character. We are like gardeners who plant seeds in the fertile earth. Add a little intellectual fertilizer, let the sun and the rain bring life to the seeds, and then we get to watch the seeds become flowers and plants and sometimes even towering trees. . . . Our greatest rewards are always intrinsic; our satisfactions come from watching a student undertake an imaginative journey or watching a youngster suddenly discover the world of ideas and thought. . . . Because we have a vocation, we put intrinsic rewards above the extrinsic rewards of salary and status. (Cookson, 2005, p. 16)

Yet it seems to me the intrinsic rewards held special importance for the educators I met. The challenges they confront are perhaps greater than most Americans truly understand. As a result, their intrinsic rewards were all the more significant and meaningful. Ultimately, it is the intrinsic rewards they found in serving Native children and reservation communities that kept them going. When I asked the teacher whose car was badly damaged by the inebriated student about the rewards in teaching, he remarked, "Well, it's not so much the pay! The pay is not really the reward!" Indeed.

I don't know what happened to the teacher's damaged car. More important, I wonder what happened to the young man who caused the damage. After meeting this educator, I have no doubt he is a man of sincerity and integrity. He is a man steeped in the cultural traditions of his people, and they regard him as an emerging elder, a preserver, and a teacher of tribal traditions. In this instance, the roles associated with serving as an educator and a tribal elder converged. I am sure this occasion provided an opportunity to perform the responsibilities of both statuses for the benefit of the young man. Only time will tell whether the student will receive and heed the instruction from the teacher, from the elder. Whatever may be the case, the teacher understood his rewards do not really come from the school district, but from the Creator.

I can still see this wise teacher as he slightly leaned forward in his chair. He took another drink of coffee and thought for a moment. Then he looked up at me, and with a mischievous smile and a quick wink, said, "Paycheck does help."

CHAPTER 5

Not Every Child Is the Same
Reservation Schools in the Era of No Child Left Behind

> *Our kids are smart. They really are. But it's the way they're tested. I don't like that because not every child is the same and that's what standardization is saying. . . . The powers that be need to acknowledge and be aware that there are other ways to determine the child's proficiency rather than just by that test.*
> —Montana principal on the No Child Left Behind policy

She kept her office neat and tidy. Although clearly a busy professional, the orderly appearance of her workspace suggested she did not allow the hectic nature of the job to overwhelm her. It didn't take us long to realize our paths had crossed some twenty years earlier. She had been a graduate student in the university where I taught upon completion of my own graduate work. Perhaps because of our common experiences and acquaintances, the interview had an even more relaxed and familiar quality than most of the meetings with the other participants.

This South Dakota principal had received many awards during her almost three decades of service, and I knew she was one of the most respected educators I would meet during my research journey. Nothing less than a veteran of many school and administrative battles, in her own words she had "seen, pretty much, it all." Her strongly held convictions had led to conflicts with higher-level administrators both in her building and in the larger district during her career. All of that did not prevent her from serving as everything from classroom teacher to principal to district administrator, earning accolades all along the way.

Eventually our conversation turned to the policy of NCLB. I was particularly interested in hearing this seasoned and respected educator's opinion on the impact of this policy. As I began my question, she looked past me and out the window in thought. She hesitated before answering, and then, with what I sensed as frustration tinged in sadness, she sighed and said,

No Child Left Behind has just changed teaching so much. I mean, assessment is the drive and it's like we are forgetting the child. No Child Left Behind, we are leaving the child behind because we have forgotten teaching styles and, like I said, the language and the culture. That has all been put on the back burner when they should actually be up front! And then you do whatever you need to do as far as instruction goes to meet those needs. The pressure has been really strong on all of our teachers and we are so data-driven right now.

As it turned out, she voiced an assessment of NCLB representative of most of the educators in this study. The prevailing view on NCLB was one of dissatisfaction and, in a few cases, even anger. It is important to note that I conducted this research before President Obama signaled the end to the NCLB policy in his 2011 State of the Union address. At this writing, the nature of any new educational policy (likely with the Race to the Top grant funds initiative as its centerpiece) remains to be seen. However, for the better part of a decade, the policy of NCLB has played a highly significant role in the professional efforts of most of the educators who participated in the study. For years, they have toiled within the mandates of NCLB and have directly witnessed its positive and negative consequences. Not surprisingly, virtually all of them voiced some opinion about the policy, the pressures of meeting adequate yearly progress (AYP) requirements, or the merits of standardized testing on which the policy relies.

This chapter examines three thorny issues associated with NCLB. First, the participants related their views on the emphasis on standardized tests, especially those required in core content areas of math and reading. Most of the educators held standardized tests in low regard and believed they do not accurately measure the abilities and knowledge of Native students. A noticeable minority disagreed with the prevailing sentiment, however, and contended that standardized testing in core content areas is necessary. Second, about half of the educators discussed the impact of NCLB on tribal cultural education. Most believed this policy has resulted in a diminished emphasis on tribal education efforts. Only a handful thought otherwise. Finally, a third of the participants brought up the pressure they felt resulting from their schools' attempts to make adequate yearly progress as mandated by NCLB. I found this especially notable because I did not initially ask about AYP. This chapter also explores some revealing differences in the views and experiences between the affinitive educators and facilitative educators on all these issues. In fact, some of the sharpest differences between these groups of professionals involve perceptions associated with the need, nature, and consequences of NCLB.

A DECADE OF NO CHILD LEFT BEHIND

In 2001 Congress passed the No Child Left Behind Act and a decade of controversy ensued. Frequently referred to simply as NCLB, the legislation intended to reduce the academic disparities evidenced in American education, most notably between whites and minorities, by making educators and schools accountable (McCarty, 2008). The policy requires that each state establish performance goals in math and reading and then to measure proficiency with standardized tests (Ravitch, 2010). These performance goals are commonly referred to as "state standards." Consequently, under NCLB students must be tested annually in the core areas of math and reading in third through eighth grade, and once in high school. It is important to bear in mind students are tested only in the core areas of math and reading and in no other subjects.

NCLB requires schools be evaluated on their performance on these tests via AYP reports. Schools failing to attain or make sufficient progress toward the state standards face severe sanctions, including a reduction in funding, reshuffling of staff, or provision of other educational options such as tuition-free education (paid for at the failing school's expense) at local high-performing schools (Forte, 2010). Therefore, it is not quite accurate to say NCLB follows a "carrot-and-stick" approach to educational reform as there is a lot more stick than carrot associated with the policy. Subsequently, educators have experienced enormous pressure to such an extent that many authorities on educational policy regard it as one of the most powerful forces shaping American education in the past fifty years (Ravitch, 2010).

The result of NCLB has been the advent of an era of "high-stakes" standardized testing in which schools and educators face enormous pressure to demonstrate student competence and proficiency. These tests are presumably objective, and thus fair, in that they consist of material uniformly presented and evaluated. Nevertheless, a significant number of scholars and practitioners challenge the alleged objectivity and fairness of standardized tests, charging they are culturally biased, easily manipulated, or poorly constructed (Forbes, 2000; Ravitch, 2010; Tienken, 2011).

The reliance on standardized testing has led to a variety of unsavory if not unethical educational practices. For instance, some have charged that NCLB encourages teachers to "teach to the test," where students are merely encouraged to inanely parrot material likely included on standardized exams rather than to strive for genuine understanding and the development of critical thinking skills (Jones, Jones, & Hargrove, 2003; Ravitch, 2010). For instance, at an annual cost of almost a billion dollars, NCLB requires early elementary grade students not meeting reading standards to participate in the Reading First reading program (McKenna & Walpole, 2010). However, some have argued this program offers highly regimented phonics instruction that largely ignores unique needs of poor and culturally or linguistically diverse students (Reyhner & Hurtado, 2008). Nevertheless, schools are mandated to use NCLB-prescribed remedies for low test scores that in effect teach to the test rather than produce genuine learning (McCarty, 2008). In this regard, Jim Cummins argues "pedagogies for the poor" have emerged under NCLB, in which "lower-income students are more likely to be taught in classroom environments where there is less opportunity to read extensively and less encouragement to engage in inquiry-oriented learning than was the case before the implementation of the 2001 No Child Left Behind (NCLB) legislation" (Cummins, 2007, p. 564).

Moreover, as a way to preempt sanctions, some have charged that schools tend to assign students not likely to meet state standards as "special education" individuals in an effort to sidestep the consequences of standardized testing results (McCarty, 2008). In particular, minority students, such as American Indian children, have suffered under this practice. The past decade witnessed the proliferation of American Indian children designated as special education students (Ingalls, Hammond, Dupoux, & Baeza, 2006).

Of special concern is the support for tribal cultural history and language subjects in the face of mounting pressures to deliver curriculum tailored to meet NCLB testing requirements (Balter & Grossman, 2009). Provisions within NCLB actually authorize the inclusion of culturally related and enriching programs. However, tribal cultural history and language courses are not part of the standardized testing included in NCLB and thus are considered to be "low-stakes" subjects. Consequently, these subjects are frequently sacrificed in favor of concentration on the "high-stakes" subjects of math and reading. This practice is known as "narrowing the curriculum"; administrators and teachers feel greater pressure to raise test scores in math and reading (Jones et al., 2003; Ravitch, 2010). As McCarty explains,

> With respect to American Indian, Alaska Native, and Native Hawaiian students, NCLB's provisions are, on the surface, reasonable, and attractive. . . . In practice these [culturally enriched] activities are highly constrained by a rigid and punitive accountability system that fails to consider improvements over previous performance, is blind to racial discrimination and attendant school funding inequalities, and uses English

standardized tests as the sole measure of proficiency. . . . Among the "low-stakes" subject matter to be sidelined are precisely those culturally related activities the law ostensibly endorses. (McCarty, 2008, p. 2)

There is a significant discussion surrounding the emphasis on standardized testing in math and reading. Namely, many argue the format and content of standardized tests tend to represent the cultural proclivities of mainstream society (Forbes, 2000). As a result, minority children, such as American Indian students, are inherently placed at a disadvantage when taking such tests (Garcia, 2008). Additionally, the enormous emphasis placed on math and reading results in the narrowing of the curriculum at the expense of other subject areas such as tribal history and language (Winstead, Lawrence, Brantmeier, & Frey, 2008). I was especially eager to understand the experiences and perceptions of the participants on this topic. I reasoned that if anyone is in a position to see the effects of NCLB-driven standardized testing in core content areas in reservation schools, surely it would be these educators, and so I asked a simple yet general question in order to explore their perspectives on issues associated with NCLB: "Based on your experience, in what ways, if any, has the emphasis on standardized tests required by NCLB impacted your school specifically or reservation schools in general?" Most of the educators displayed strong reactions to the question. Their responses tended to focus on two general issues: First, most of them offered their thoughts on the merits of standardized tests as an assessment tool. Second, a smaller number of the participants addressed the impact of NCLB-driven standardized testing on tribal cultural education in their schools.

Standardized Testing and Assessment

Only four of the participants displayed ambivalent views on NCLB and did not indicate one way or another whether that participant believed standardized testing to be appropriate or inappropriate as an assessment technique, whereas seventeen of the educators did express specific opinions on the merits of standardized testing mandated by NCLB. A few of the educators regarded standardized testing as necessary. Most of them did not. Indeed, a couple of the educators became indignant and angry during the interview. In the opinion of these individuals, NCLB with its required standardized testing in math and reading has created a number of negative consequences for Native children and reservation schools.

The majority of educators emphatically declared that standardized testing is an inappropriate assessment device. Twelve of the twenty-one educators (nine affinitive and three facilitative) specifically expressed the view that standardized testing does not fairly or accurately measure the knowledge and abilities of their students. Typical of this opinion is a Montana educator who related,

> I firmly believe that standardized testing is really inaccurate. I truly believe we are not getting a clear picture of how well our students learn, of their learning styles and how they perceive things. I mean, when we have to teach to the test I don't believe we are doing our kids justice. It's really challenging at times because, for example, you ask them a question on a math test and they can verbally tell you the answer. The language is there, the comprehension of the question is there. But you give that same question on a test and it's like it just goes out the window.

Some of the educators criticized standardized tests for their failure to recognize the cultural distinctiveness of Native children. Most notable in this regard are language and vernacular differences found on reservations. For instance, a Montana principal contended,

> What I find is that on the national tests, or our statewide tests even, is that if you talk to our kids they may be able to answer the question. Things that trip them up are vocabulary and the different vernacular that are used on the tests. But if you spoke the way they know, then, "Oh, I can answer that." So I think it's not going to show what they know. And another thing I find is we're not showing what we know because we're being given a test that we may or may not understand due to our vocabulary, due to where we live. Because I think not only do they have a different language, there is a certain language here on the reservation.

A number of the educators related that pervasive social problems such as poverty and problematic family situations make it difficult for students to perform well on standardized tests. As a result, reservation schools have great difficulty making AYP. A Montana principal explained simply, "Today almost every reservation school in Montana isn't making AYP. Give me a break. You know why it is. There's so many problems here."

One Montana educator attributed the poor performance on standardized testing to the combined effects of cultural discrepancies and the social conditions found on the reservation. In this view, standardized tests are designed by and for those representing vastly different social classes and cultural experiences and, therefore, cannot possibly measure the true abilities of most reservation children:

> All I know about standardization is it just doesn't give a picture of what our kids really know. I mean, that's a difficult thing. We are talking about low-income kids. I mean, what is on those tests and what our kids know just doesn't mesh. . . . Our kids are knowledgeable, but they don't perform and it's a performance thing. And there are some cultural things within there. Because what is important in this locale isn't necessarily what is being tested on in that particular test. We do infuse a lot of Indian Education for All [a Montana state initiative requiring Native American culture and history be included across the curriculum in all schools] and those kinds of things and they don't test that there.

A couple of the educators became quite angry while discussing NCLB and standardized testing. These individuals were greatly frustrated by the depiction of Native children they believe results from standardized tests scores. They also were bitter about the potential punitive measures threatening reservation schools. Mixing sarcasm with resentment, one Montana educator pointed out the irony over political rhetoric claiming to value diversity against the reality of NCLB's insistence that all students be tested and scored in a standardized fashion. He argued, "Even though we are in America and everyone is supposed to be different we are going to glump it all together. And these are the things that everybody should know. And it's not so much a priority here. And I would even venture to say that those types of standards are not only going to hurt here, but harm most of rural America because the standards are being built for places that are not rural."

An even more powerful indictment came from a Montana principal. During the interview, his pent-up frustration with the mandates of NCLB and the looming threats over his school's failure to make AYP burst forth. His school had suffered a series of recent student suicides and the pain of the tragedies had pushed many at the school, including the principal, near the emotional breaking point. These events provide some context for his anger:

> Initially when I got my master's that [NCLB mandates] was sort of shoved down my throat. But I was sort of naïve in believing that because I grew up here and I lived this. I've seen a lot of things outsiders don't get to see and I can tell you this: No Child Left Behind is really nothing but a joke. I think our kids—I love our kids—and a lot of our kids will never be at that level where they want them to be. But that doesn't mean my kids are stupid and when this stuff comes out it makes our kids look like they are stupid. And that really makes me angry because they're not! All it is to me is nothing more than a political grandstand for people to say we are doing something.

The charge that standardized testing is an inappropriate assessment approach for Native students is hardly new. Even before the enactment of NCLB, scholars had cautioned against the propriety of standardized tests (Van Hamme, 1996). None, perhaps, has been more frank about the agenda driving standardized testing and the push for nationalized curriculum standards than Jack Forbes. Writing a year before NCLB was presented before Congress, Forbes argued,

> [T]here is reason to believe that the push for "standards" is actually an attempt to destroy multiculturalism, pluralism, and non-Anglo ethnic-specific curriculum by forcing all public schools to adhere to a curriculum approved by centralized agencies controlled by white people. The standards are to be enforced by means of constant testing of students (and often of teachers) based solely on the centrally approved curriculum.... What standardized tests surely do is to force upon states, localities, and regions a collectivist "testing culture" that negates the unique heritages, dialects, and values of a particular area. Native nations and the schools serving their pupils will most likely become as assimilationistic as the pre-1928 BIA [Bureau of Indian Affairs] boarding and mission schools. (Forbes, 2000, p. 8)

While the prevailing view among the participants held that NCLB-driven standardized tests are inappropriate assessments for Native children, there were those who disagreed. Six of the educators (one of the affinitive and five of the facilitative) regarded standardized tests as necessary. These educators typically believed standardized tests measure the basic knowledge skills necessary for success in life. Therefore, it is important for educators to understand the academic strengths and weaknesses of reservation children in order to prepare them for the future. However, even those educators who regarded standardized testing as necessary for assessment disagreed about the nature of the tests and the practice of testing in only two core areas. Three of the individuals welcomed the chance to have their students take standardized tests and anticipated the results, while three others indicated ambivalence about such exams but nevertheless accepted their necessity. A Montana educator explained her views on standardized testing:

> I just feel we are going to have to meet them [NCLB associated state standards]. But what is difficult is that they keep raising [the standards] and even if we are making a little progress ... I don't see how they can successfully make it in college if they don't have good writing skills.... But we have to rise to the standards because that is the only way that we will survive and continue to survive with the outside world. Because

we have to have educated people and I just think that somewhere in those tests they are saying you need these skills to be successful at the next level.

A South Dakota elementary teacher expressed her anticipation of standardized tests results. For this educator, standardized tests represent a way to demonstrate the capabilities of reservation children:

> I just want to see an improvement. . . . I push my [students] hard. I work them every day. We are busy, busy bodies. Next year, my first group will be in third grade. I want to see if there is a difference. You know what I mean? I want to be able to research that and see what their testing is like. . . . This is their beginning. I need to do my best to get them ready as readers, as writers. You know, get them started. So I am really going to be interested in seeing [the testing results] next year. I am hopeful.

During one of the interviews, a South Dakota high school teacher displayed tremendous indignation over the implication that Native students are not capable of performing on standardized tests. This educator's comments reveal that, in her estimation, standardized tests are important to document the academic proficiency of Native students:

> People can say, "Oh standardized tests are geared towards white, middle-class males" or whatever. I did very well on standardized tests. I am neither male nor white. And a lot of people will stand up and proclaim, "Well, it doesn't pertain to our Native students!" Yeah, it does because it's just basic knowledge. All we need is that basic knowledge. That's all these students need. This is just one thing that drives me crazy. The one excuse is, "Well they're Native students." Kids are kids. It doesn't matter what color they are.

Three of the educators voiced less-sanguine views about standardized testing. They accepted the inevitability of standardized tests as assessment techniques without necessarily endorsing them. For instance, a South Dakota educator remarked, "No Child Left Behind is here regardless of what we as educators do and there are certain standards that we have to meet. . . . The reality is we have to do what the state is telling us. We have to get those scores up." Similarly, a Montana principal offered, "I don't like the standardization. I used to cringe every time that came around. But I do believe that in order for our students to be successful in both cultures they need to be able to take those tests, too, because they're not going to go away. I mean, they're going to be here. And I think as teachers, or as educators, we need to focus [on] or expose our children to more of those test-type questions and to teach them how to respond to them."

Whatever else one may think about the issue, the culture of American education includes standardized testing as an entrenched form of assessment. It is unlikely that policymakers and educational leaders will discontinue using standardized test scores to make inferences about student, teacher, and school performance, yet many scholars share the concerns expressed by a significant number of the participants in this study. In fact, one of the most persistent criticisms of NCLB relates to the propriety of using standardized tests to evaluate instructional effectiveness and learning outcomes for Native and other minority children (Altshuler & Schmautz, 2006; Hood, 1998; Nelson-Barber & Trumbull, 2007).

Given the chorus of criticism, one might find it somewhat surprising that six of the educators specifically related that they believe NCLB-mandated standardized testing is necessary. It should be noted that five of these six were facilitative educators. Thus, the contrast between affinitive educators and facilitative educators is revealing. Simply put, the majority of affinitive educators described standardized testing as an inappropriate form of assessment, and the majority of facilitative educators believed they are necessary. Yet even among these perceptions there is greater complexity than a casual observation would suggest. A closer examination of their perceptions and experiences reveals that the half of the educators who related that standardized tests are necessary (including two facilitative educators) did not necessarily advocate for these assessment techniques as much as they were simply resigned to their usage. They regarded standardized tests as a way to gauge student knowledge and skills necessary for postmodern society but also displayed ambivalence about the costs of undue emphasis on these kinds of assessments. Affinitive educators and facilitative educators held different perceptions on standardized tests, yet they shared many of the same experiences. Unlike affinitive educators, facilitative educators believed standardized test are necessary. Nevertheless, like their affinitive colleagues, many facilitative educators struggled with the frustration and anxiety produced by their continued use.

Standardized Tests and Tribal Cultural Education

Going into the research I expected the participants would have a great deal to say on the issue of standardized testing and tribal cultural education. By tribal cultural education, I mean a combination of culturally relevant pedagogical practices, infusion of tribal values and worldview into academic subject matter, and specific tribal culture and language curriculum. In other words, "tribal cultural education" is a generic term I use to refer to a number of educational approaches designed to enhance children's understanding and appreciation of their tribal heritage and identity. Ten of the participants, virtually half, specifically mentioned the impact of standardized testing in core content areas on tribal cultural educational efforts. The majority of these educators believed the emphasis of standardized testing in the core subjects of math and reading has negatively impacted tribal cultural education subjects taught in their schools. However, a few of the educators contended that the prominence placed on standardized testing in core subjects has not adversely affected tribal education efforts.

Ten educators (seven of the affinitive educators and three of the facilitative educators) argued tribal cultural education has suffered as a result of the increased emphasis on core area subjects of math and reading. For instance, a Montana educator contended the urgency of making AYP deflects emphasis from tribal cultural education efforts. He reflected, "I think we would love for our school to be just filled with their traditions and the culture and the language but you can't do it because you're fighting an educational system that says this needs to happen, you know, AYP, improvement. I think one of the ways to do it [make academic gains] is really to devote a lot of your schedule and a lot of your resources to a traditional way of life. But that will never happen."

Offering a virtually identical view, a South Dakota principal explained the drive among reservation schools to make AYP has greatly diminished their efforts to offer tribal cultural education:

> When I first started, there was a lot of integration of [name of tribe] culture and language. We had grants where we had Title III staff and I had Title VII teachers who knew the language and they went into the classroom and they also worked with the teacher to integrate the culture. But that is gone. I mean, almost every classroom had those types of teachers. Now in the district we only have four. . . . But that hasn't been our drive with NCLB. It's been reading, math, and making sure we do what we have to do. So we've lost that and now we have to try to bring it back somehow. . . . You can't be so rigid that you lose how a Native child learns. And I believe they learn differently. You have to have a strong relationship with them, you have to have humor in the classroom, you have to have collaborative learning going on. Those things have to be in place. You can't just have kids sitting in rows regurgitating information. It's not going to happen.

While discussing the biggest challenges she has faced as an educator on the reservation, a South Dakota principal identified the reduction in the number of tribal-oriented subjects that she claimed has resulted from the pressures of NCLB. She especially resented the outside interference in the education of reservation children:

> The changes in education and NCLB is one of them [the challenges associated with teaching on the reservation]. As a Native leader, I feel like I really know what Native children need and we have moved so far away from the culture and the language when we should have been looking more at where these kids are coming from when they come into the classroom. We should be setting up our schools for their culture, not outsiders coming and saying, "Okay, this is the culture. You have to perform and you have to produce." That has been the strongest challenge.

The participants in this study are not alone in their concerns. Balter and Grossman (2009) found Navajo educators also reported feeling restricted in their efforts to offer tribal cultural subjects (most notably language acquisition courses) as a result of the pressures produced by NCLB's required standardized testing policy. Despite the fact the educators in their study generally supported NCLB's effort to concentrate on the needs of students, many of their respondents reported they have had to abandon culturally relevant pedagogical practices in order to prepare students for standardized tests in math and reading. Balter and Grossman (2009) conclude, "Because Navajo language and culture are facing extinction, such a curricular shift may be culturally catastrophic" (p. 19).

Nevertheless, three participants (one affinitive and two facilitative educators) did not believe the emphasis on standardized testing diminishes efforts to provide tribal cultural education in their schools. Unfortunately, even when I probed for elaboration, two of the educators offered little explanation for their opinions. Only one of these individuals, a Montana educator, engaged in extended discussion on why he believed standardized testing does not deter from tribal cultural education efforts. This individual did not see a contradiction between stressing the core standards incorporated under NCLB and infusing tribal culture into daily instruction. Rather, he believed that with innovation and hard work teachers can overcome difficulties imposed by a greater emphasis on standardized testing in math and reading:

> I feel that you can teach the standards and you can have the culture. There are ways to incorporate both. You need dynamic people and you need dynamic ideas to do that and it takes more work. . . . I mean, I teach standards and I push my kids towards standards. You know, evaluation, fact and opinion, and sequencing—you can incor-

porate culture into those. It just takes some planning and it takes some work. . . . I see the argument where they say that the culture is under attack. Well, the culture has already been attacked and in many communities the culture has been decimated to a point where it's hard to recognize what was there 150 years ago. But I don't see the push toward national standardization as an attack on culture when you can bring culture in and teach standards. It just takes some work.

The perceptions of the participants come down to two basic points of view. On the one hand, there are those, mostly affinitive educators, who hold that the emphasis on standardized testing in core content areas unequivocally damages tribal cultural education efforts in schools. On the other hand, the other view, held by only a few educators, maintains the emphasis on standardized testing does not necessarily undermine tribal cultural education in reservation schools.

More than anything else, the perceptions related by the participants indicate a genuine uneasiness with the state of tribal cultural education. By and large, they regarded tribal cultural education as a fragile component of the school's mission and subsequently displayed a great deal of frustration. Most recognized the crucial importance of tribal cultural education in all its various expressions, including cultural responsive teaching approaches and tribal language and history subjects. But they also recognized how easily tribal cultural education (something over which they exercise a measure of control) can be made the proverbial stepchild to educational policy mandates (something over which they have no realistic control). The situation invites frustration and anxiety. The conclusion reached by Nelson-Barber and Trumbull (2007) likely describes the views held by the majority of the educators I interviewed: "It is not just the inappropriateness of the tests themselves but also the ways they affect the entire educational process that must concern [us]. . . . The unfortunate outcome of NCLB legislation may well be that educators of Native students must move further away from culturally congruent curriculum, instruction, and assessment rather than increasing their use—despite all the evidence of their value" (p. 134).

Pressure Striving for Adequate Yearly Progress

The Bush administration and Congress intended the 2001 No Child Left Behind Act to create systems of accountability for American schools and educators (Linn, Baker, & Betebenner, 2002). In order to measure student progress (and presumably school quality), the legislation mandated a system to evaluate performance. Toward that end, NCLB requires annual reports of standardized tests scores on mathematics and reading, officially known as adequate yearly progress, or simply AYP. As mentioned previously, repeated failure to meet the minimal levels of proficiency established by the state can result in a number of punitive measures. As a result, AYP has become the coin of the realm during the NCLB era. Consequently, throughout the past decade school personnel have experienced great pressure to meet AYP. Nowhere has this pressure been more intensely experienced than in schools serving low-income, high-poverty populations or rural populations, ironically the very schools NCLB seeks to assist (Forte, 2010; Mitchem, Kossar, & Ludlow, 2006).

Although I did not ask about AYP during the interviews, a third of the participants (five affinitive and two facilitative educators) specifically mentioned the pressure associated with striving to make AYP. I should also note that in subsequent inquiries I discovered none of the schools I visited was making AYP—a situation, unfortunately, not uncommon among reservation schools (Zehr, 2007).

A Montana teacher addressed the perplexing struggle to make AYP at her school. She described the frustration she and others experience:

> I think that most teachers do the best they possibly can and I don't understand how they can say that a teacher is not trying to do their best. I mean, let's get rid of all of them or let's do a shake-up and put that one in kindergarten, and this one in third, and so on and so forth. And that just makes pressure on the teacher. The students don't do as well because the teacher is so stressed out in the first place about it. . . . Once you reach your safe harbor, then you have to have a higher level, you know it has to be more! Instead of 70 percent it has to be 90 percent. If you're just barely struggling to meet the first level, why do you have to go up a level again? It's really frustrating to me.

A South Dakota principal became visibly downcast when addressing AYP:

> I don't agree with it [No Child Left Behind]. It has some good things attached to it—accountability. And teachers need to be accountable. I totally agree with that. They don't look at us as who we are or our needs. To me, kids need to know who they are first. And that's all there is to it. And what's unfair about that is there is only one test we get graded on and we have yet to make AYP. We make gains but not enough because they raise the bar every year. And it's disheartening when we get that school report card. I hate that.

A Montana principal spoke with remarkable candor about his school's failure to make AYP. For this educator, the insistence on making AYP had created an unethical system of rewards and punishments. More seriously, it had also resulted in an educational system in which teachers focus on the more proficient students at the expense of the struggling students: "I think when you talk about No Child Left Behind, I think it's geared towards helping your top, your AYP, your proficient, and your advanced kids to be more proficient and more advanced and it's hurting your novice and your lower-end kids because really what it is doing is causing educators to pick and choose who is going to improve their scores most. . . . We haven't made AYP. I've been here for eleven years and will we ever make AYP under the current system? I don't think we will."

Later in the interview he displayed a great deal of frustration over the lack of recognition of the serious social and family conditions that, in his opinion, inhibit reservation schools from making strides toward AYP:

> You know, I think me being here is about that much [uses his fingers to indicate a small amount] of what a parent can do. I think a parent who is truly involved and who wants to be involved, who doesn't drink and bring alcohol into the home and drugs, can affect their kid so much more. I really get tired of the feds and whoever knocking our schools because we don't make AYP and trying to figure out what the answer is. I know what the answer is. They want to keep saying that you didn't improve instruction. Well, that's not the answer.

Researchers have documented how the pressures associated with striving for AYP exacts a heavy cost on the morale of teachers serving high-poverty schools (Byrd-Blake et al., 2010). It is easy to understand why. Many educators resent the top-down mandates imposed on them. Those mandates, it should be noted, have little to no local support. One public opinion poll revealed that merely 15 percent of those surveyed believe local education has improved since the implementation of NCLB (Hargreaves & Shirley, 2008). The frustration for the participants is compounded by the fact that the majority of them do not even trust the accuracy of the tests, yet the reputations of individual professionals and entire schools rest upon test results.

However, the discrepancy displayed by affinitive educators and facilitative educators is notable. Nearly half of the affinitive educators volunteered their frustrations with AYP but only two facilitative educators related similar experiences. This is a revealing pattern in the experiences of these educators, but does it also mean that affinitive educators experience greater pressure resulting from AYP? Perhaps it does and, just as easily, perhaps it does not. What it could indicate is that affinitive educators were more willing to freely express their frustrations while facilitative educators (who stressed the importance of professional competence) were simply less inclined to spontaneously discuss feeling pressured due to AYP.

COMPARISON OF AFFINITIVE EDUCATORS AND FACILITATIVE EDUCATORS

Affinitive educators and facilitative educators evidenced notable differences in their respective views on issues associated with NCLB. Affinitive educators were more likely to express apprehension over standardized testing compared to facilitative educators. Whereas nine of the twelve affinitive educators regarded standardized testing as inappropriate forms of assessment, only three of the nine facilitative educators expressed similar objections. Also, whereas only one of the affinitive educators considered standardized tests as necessary, five of the facilitative educators believed in the necessity of such assessments.

An additional difference appears in how they regarded the impact of standardized testing on the tribal cultural education efforts in their schools. Compared to facilitative educators, affinitive educators were more likely to convey misgivings about NCLB. In fact, whereas seven of the twelve affinitive educators discussed the negative impact of NCLB policies on tribal cultural education, only three of the nine facilitative expressed such concerns. Simply put, the affinitive educators were more likely to deem the emphasis placed on standardized testing in core content areas as diminishing the focus on tribal cultural education efforts.

Finally, the educators in this study differed in their respective concerns over making AYP. A larger proportion of affinitive educators described pressures to achieve AYP than did facilitative educators. Five of the twelve affinitive educators and only two of the nine facilitative educators described the difficulty and strain associated with striving to make AYP.

The difference in views between affinitive educators and facilitative educators result from a number of factors. How they considered their role as educators must surely shape their attitudes toward standardized tests and AYP. Perhaps facilitative educators, who highly esteemed professional competency, were not as put off by efforts to objectively measure student proficiency compared with the affinitive educators. Indeed, such approaches to appraise student proficiency and, by extension, teacher competency are consistent with their basic philosophy as educators. Given the general nature of the comments provided by facilitative educators, it seems to me they objected less to the principle of holding teachers accountable and the measurement of student proficiency than they did to what they considered to be the heavy-handed nature of NCLB.

Affinitive educators, on the other hand, valued the personal relationships they build with students. These educational professionals believed learning must first derive and build from interpersonal relationships. Moreover, they judged establishing personal connections with students as especially important when teaching Native children, and they found highly formalized standardized tests particularly repulsive, objecting to their impersonal, overly rationalized nature. Furthermore, as a number of them pointed out, affinitive educators generally believed standardized tests simply do not capture the true academic proficiency of their students. They knew their students were academically capable because of their personal, ongoing interactions with them. The real problem lies in the inability of standardized tests to document the true knowledge level of Native students. Ultimately, the educators resented the pressure to make AYP when they considered the measurement devices themselves as flawed.

Another possible reason for the difference between affinitive educators and facilitative educators relates to their respective backgrounds. Affinitive educators, more so than facilitative educators, came from culturally traditional backgrounds. Half of them were fluent Native speakers. Perhaps these individuals were especially alert to any effort that could diminish tribal cultural education for Native children. I do not mean to imply that facilitative educators placed less value on tribal traditions than did affinitive educators. Indeed, this would be a grossly unfair and inaccurate conclusion. However, the nature of the cultural background common to many affinitive educators might have predisposed them to be more sensitive to assaults on tribal cultural training.

It is also interesting that among the ten individuals concerned about the diminishing focus on tribal cultural education efforts, nine were from South Dakota and only one was from Montana. This is a potentially important pattern because Montana requires what is known as Indian Education for All. Although it took more than three decades to implement, under Montana state law all schools in the state, both on and off the reservations, must infuse American Indian culture and history into the curriculum (Juneau & Smoker Broaddus, 2006). Moreover, Indian Education for All proposes educators integrate American Indian cultural and historical content with standards-based instruction in all curricular areas (Kelting-Gibson, 2006; Ngai & Koehn, 2010; Pember, 2007).

Possibly Indian Education for All helped ameliorate the misgivings among the Montana educators over a loss of emphasis on American Indian education. South Dakota educators, on the other hand, served in schools without such educational provisions. Therefore, they were more likely to distress over a lack of emphasis on American Indian culture and history. Simply put, perhaps the South Dakota educators had a greater reason to be concerned about the lack of emphasis on American Indian cultural education in their schools.

CONCLUSION

A number of scholars claim NCLB represents the most ambitious attempt at educational reform in our nation's history (Noguera, 2010; Ravitch, 2010). It is also one of the most controversial efforts at educational reform. The storm surrounding it is so great that Congressman George Miller of California called NCLB "the most tainted brand in America" (Jennings, 2011, p. 44). Ironically, Representative Miller was also one of the principal sponsors of the original bill.

Like most reforms, NCLB began with noble intentions and lofty goals. Essentially, NCLB sought to ensure that all of the nation's children would be educated to meet high academic standards and that those providing their education would be held accountable. Such ambitious objectives invite far-reaching political rhetoric that promises a great deal. As Diane Ravitch (2010) observes, "School reformers sometimes resemble the characters in Dr. Seuss's *Solla Sollew,* who are always searching for that mythical land 'where they never have troubles, at least very few'" (p. 3). Unfortunately, a complicated policy such as NCLB guarantees a lot of troubles as well as an equal amount of controversy (Darling-Hammond, 2007).

As far as an educational policy is concerned, our national search for the mythical land where troubles are few has come up short once again, but it will not prevent us from continuing to search. One thing is certain: scholars and policymakers will study and analyze the impact of NCLB for years to come. Much like the War on Poverty of forty years ago, it will be held up for ridicule by some while regarded as a naïvely ambitious but nonetheless noble policy by others. What is more, just as the War on Poverty serves as a demarcation point in American social welfare policy, NCLB may well represent a watershed in American educational policy. From this point forward, we may never think of student academic proficiency and school accountability in exactly the same ways as before NCLB.

Like so many other American educators, reservation teachers and principals have found themselves in the middle of the conundrum created by the

NCLB policy. The participants in this study revealed deep frustrations and anxiety as a result. Whatever policy eventually replaces NCLB, it will most assuredly bring its own set of difficulties. The truth is that reservation educators face an added complexity shared by some but not all teachers in mainstream schools. American Indian educators must not only meet the educational demands required by students in order to prepare them for life in a postmodern society, but also frequently must assist elders in preserving the culture of their peoples by providing tribal cultural education. The same South Dakota principal introduced at the beginning of this chapter who lamented the reduced emphasis on tribal cultural education resulting from the demands of NCLB also stated, "We are slowly bringing the culture back in. In the morning, we have gatherings in which the kids gather outside and they get into drum and get themselves ready for the day. There's little things we are starting to bring back into the district besides the push for success. And we are seeing growth. But it's so slow." I understand her frustration and admire her determination. Slow progress, I suppose, is better than no progress.

CHAPTER 6

Spread Like Wildfire
Importance of American Indian Educators

> *One of the elders there said, "The news of you getting hired has spread like wildfire through our community. We're so happy you're here. In all our whole history of the school system, we have never had an Indian administrator."*
> —*Montana educator, on being named principal of a reservation school*

I had never been to this particular reservation before and could not help but notice the lonely white crosses, typically adorned with small tributes, dotting the side of the road. Memorials to loved ones lost in traffic accidents. On one ten-mile stretch of the highway, I counted almost twenty crosses, nearly one cross every half mile. The crosses appeared more frequently as I neared my destination. Curious about what I had seen during the morning, after concluding all the interviews on that first day I drove a few miles out the other side of the town and witnessed a virtually identical pattern of crosses along the side of the road. It reminded me of a battlefield.

The sad memorials give testimony to a harsh reality of reservation life. In many respects this reservation, like so many others, is a battlefield, and has been one for some time. The centuries of relentless and dreadful assault endured by American Indians resulted in unimaginable loss of life, land, and culture. Even today, ancient wisdom continues to be lost and entire languages forever silenced. In his now classic book *The Sociological Imagination*, C. Wright Mills (1959) distinguished between private *troubles* and public *issues*. For Mills, troubles include the personal problems plaguing the lives of individuals and are part of everyday life. Conversely, issues affect large numbers of people and result from historical events and social structural arrangements. The sociological imagination allows a person to see the connection between troubles and issues. That is, personal troubles frequently have their origin in the larger social history of the group and, thus, are part of the public issues facing society. I did not have to put my sociological imagination in overdrive to see the link between private troubles and public issues on this reservation. Many, if not most, of the little white crosses I saw during my visit to that Montana reservation directly resulted from the quiet holocaust of cultural loss. Personal calamities of alienation, depression, alcoholism, drug abuse, suicide, child neglect, and drunk driving all provide sad witness that cultural loss exacts a terrible toll. American Indians remain embattled peoples.

Arriving in the dusty little town, I quickly found the school. It looked larger than I expected for such a small community. Laid out in a one-story L-shape, by all outward appearances the school would be largely indistinguishable from any other school in rural America. That perception changed once I walked into the building. Clearly, this school was designed to serve American Indian children. It reflected the students' tribal heritage in its décor and atmosphere.

The participant and I sat in the school's cultural resource room. Although quite a large room, it had a comfortable, inviting ambience. The staff had filled the room with star quilts, artwork, and posters celebrating Native traditions and leaders. Comfortable couches, coffee tables, soft chairs, and a library rounded out the area.

The participant had more than twenty years experience educating American Indian youth on the reservation and strongly believed in the need for greater numbers of American Indian educators. She also believed reservation schools need dedicated non-Native teachers, and that students require the ability to relate to all kinds of different people. She felt culturally sensitive and caring non-Native educators can provide invaluable service. I found her views on schools and tribal culture especially significant. She was preparing to assume a new position as principal of another reservation school and she spoke of her vision and philosophy for the new assignment:

> I see star quilts. I see artwork. I see staff responding positively to students. I see displays that showcase their tribal heritage, their tribal culture. And the school in [the community where she was going to be principal] there's nothing. . . . If you can't make it culturally relative to what these kids know, it's not going to stick with them. And that's what Indian education is all about, infusing education with your culture. . . . And I think that's the key. . . . I just think it's important to teach our Native children that it is possible to be bicultural and you almost have to be if you plan on going to a college. And it's not always going to be easy. It hardly ever is for Indian people.

Like so many others, this participant recognized that because formal education had long been used as a weapon in the assault on indigenous cultures, many American Indian people still regard schools with suspicion or indifference. Unfortunately, the current emphasis on standardized tests as the virtual lone measure of student proficiency has not changed the minds of critics who believe the manifest function of schools remains the cultural assimilation of Native children (Forbes, 2000).

NATIVE EDUCATORS AND RESERVATION COMMUNITIES

During the interviews, I asked the participants for suggestions on ways reservation communities might develop a larger number of Native educators. Our conversations went far beyond that question to other important matters. They wanted me to know not only how reservations can encourage larger numbers of American Indian educators, but also why they should. This chapter presents the views of the participants on three interrelated issues. The individuals I met held strong views on the importance of American Indian educators serving in reservation schools, the different ways reservation communities can increase the number of American Indian teachers and administrators, and how grounding in tribal culture makes them more effective as professional educators. Moreover, the affinitive educators and facilitative educators evidenced some of the closest views on these issues. Simply put, there is no real difference among the two kinds of educators on the importance of Native educators, on approaches to increase the number of Native educators, or on the appropriation of professional effectiveness from tribal cultural strengths.

Importance of American Indian Educators

According to Thomas Peacock (2006), more than anything else American Indian students respond to a teacher's knowledge of tribal culture. Peacock, it should be noted, is one of the nation's most preeminent authorities on teacher preparation for those who plan to serve American Indian students. Such an assertion coming from Peacock underscores the importance of American Indian educators. Perhaps not surprisingly, therefore, the majority of the participants spoke of the need for American Indian educators serving reservation students and the advantages they have over non-Native educators. Several of them qualified their remarks by stating reservation schools do not merely need American Indian educators, but also need high-quality Native teachers and administrators. As the Montana principal introduced at the beginning of this chapter pronounced, "I think it's very important [to have American

Indian educators] in the respect that they are living role models—positive role models. But not just Native teachers, I would take that one step further—quality Native teachers. . . . Not everybody can be a teacher because you got to have the heart and the will. You can't just put kids on autopilot and expect them to be successful. But I think it's very important to have quality Native teachers. Very important!"

Another Montana educator suggested reservations need more American Indian administrators as well as teachers. She contended because Native administrators understand the unique conditions found on reservations and the needs of Native children, they are more likely to make appropriate decisions: "We do need more Native American administrators. I think they would make a difference in making better decisions for our kids because some just say, 'Okay, you got a write-up. Okay, one, two, three, you're out!' You know, set in stone. They don't look at why these things happen. Why are they acting out in class? Why, when we could try to work with this kid? His home life is not very good. Let's not drive them away from school. Let's try to keep them in school."

The majority of the educators believe American Indian educators have inherent advantages compared to non-Native educators. Indeed, fourteen of the twenty-one participants specifically stated American Indian educators have advantages not necessarily possessed by non-Natives. Moreover, affinitive educators and facilitative educators expressed comparable views on this issue. Eight of the twelve affinitive educators and six of the nine facilitative agreed that American Indian educators have advantages not enjoyed by non-Native educators.

The participants outlined the kinds of advantages for Native educators, but they also discussed the reasons why American Indian educators have certain advantages. A common contention holds American Indian students and community residents simply prefer and relate better to American Indian educators. A South Dakota elementary teacher described her advantages as a Native educator:

> I think they [students] respond to me more because I am [American Indian tribe]. And even discipline—all I have to do is look at them or make a body gesture and they know, "Oh yeah, I've got to behave." Even to say one [tribal language] word. . . . I think I am a role model. The families know me, the parents know me, the communities know me. So I think I have a big impact on them. I think they wish there were more Native American teachers. More [tribal] teachers. . . . I'm not just a teacher. I'm

a [American Indian tribe] woman and a friend. Somebody they can trust and depend on if they need help.

She explained the reason for her advantage:

> There's a connection there and I guess I'm lucky that way. They say the non-Indian teachers really don't get out there [in the community] like they should. I don't know why, if it's because they are scared. . . . I think they [parents] don't feel welcome because the non-Indian teachers don't make that effort to be visible. Even if we have basketball games or whatever, they won't even go. . . . They [parents] look to us more. They respect us more because we're visible, we're out there, and we're making the effort to contact them and bring them in and make them feel welcome. I think we have more of an impact. They [non-Native educators] have to earn the respect.

A South Dakota teacher also contended people in the community simply trust American Indian educators more than they do non-Native educators. In her view, Native educators' greater inclination to participate in the community serves to legitimize them in the eyes of parents as well as students. This is especially the case for educators charged with teaching tribal cultural subjects. She explained, "I know I am trusted. . . . I have had many parental requests and I know almost everybody here. . . . To effectively teach the [American Indian tribe] culture you have to be involved in the community and become part of it. I am really a strong believer in that. And once you do that, you start living it and teaching it."

Likewise, a Montana principal believed trust is a major issue facing non-Native educators in reservation schools. He recounted, "There's definitely trust issues with outside people. They just say it's another person coming through our system. And that's just what it is. There are many talented people who have come in here, great educators, great people. But they always have to overcome that. They kind of want to test you, they don't trust you."

A Montana educator made an interesting observation about how people often perceive non-Native educators. He suggests some non-Native educators, especially those new to the community, frequently display an arrogant attitude that ultimately renders them ineffective: "I think that a [non-Native] person who just came in here there would be a difference [in effectiveness]. Because just through what the community has seen and thinks is that sometimes when people come here they'll listen and try and help but they are listening and helping because they think they can do it better or they can save somebody. . . . I think on a reservation school there's a fine line to walk between coming in and being the savior and coming in and just really doing the things and understanding how things are played out."

A South Dakota principal felt much the same way about the attitudes of some non-Native educators. During the interview she, too, discussed negative experiences with a few non-Native educators:

> Anyone who comes on the reservation needs to really know and understand that our students have a lot going against them but they are very resilient and they are very caring. You really have to know the people and you have to understand what works for Native American children. I've seen kids resist authority when you have people come in and be cold and [say], "You're going to do it this way and no other way." That's when trouble happens. You really have to understand the students and know where they are coming from. Have that sensitivity and be human.

Some of the educators indicated American Indian teachers serve as natural role models, and thus they can build the personal connections necessary for effective instruction. A Montana principal related such a view when he said, "Not only can you relate with kids in a way that most people can't, but there's something about dark skin working in reservations they think that, 'Well, cool, this guy is one of me, he's part of me, he's who I am.' There's a relationship that gets built, I think, that doesn't get built with non-Native teachers."

In the estimation of one South Dakota teacher, American Indian educators do have an advantage over non-Native educators. However, she quickly added that a number of factors complicate any advantages possessed by Native educators. This individual, who I treated as a facilitative educator, stressed the importance of providing effective academic preparation for students: "I do think they [American Indian educators] do [have an advantage] but I don't think it necessarily makes them better educators. We have had Native teachers here who I think were horrible educators. They could connect with the kids but as far as an education goes, they failed. They were focusing way too much on making that cultural connection. And sometimes I think that we give our kids too many outs because we know where they came from and our expectations are lower because we know their backgrounds." She continued by explaining how initially she deliberately emphasizes her role as an educator, and only later constructs personal relationships based on her racial connection with students:

> They look at me differently [because she is American Indian] but I don't want them to judge me as an educator based on that. I don't want them to be like, "Oh we like

[participant's name] because she is Native." Because there's not all Native teachers here. That's not reality, that they are always going to come into contact with educators or bosses that are all Native. I want them to judge me on being their teacher as a human being, that I am fair with them, before they decide that I'm Native. I don't use it to my advantage. I am sure some teachers do. I just prefer that they get to know me [as a teacher] first before they get to know anything about my background.

Only two participants specifically stated they do not believe American Indian educators have any particular inherent advantage over non-Native educators. One, a Montana teacher, simply stated, "I think that kids are the same pretty much everywhere. Except our kids need a little bit more attention." A South Dakota educator personalized this issue by relating that his racial status does not offer any special advantage. This individual was not originally from the reservation where he served and, in fact, belongs to a different tribe. His response illustrates the marginality he likely felt as a relative newcomer to the school and reservation: "I don't believe it [being an American Indian educator] has made an impact. I really don't. And that's strange in a sense. I would think it would. But no one has said, 'You're Native. I'm glad you're here. You understand some of the problems that are going on.' I've lived on a reservation and I know some of the issues. So in that sense I don't know if I am making that big of an impression to them. I don't see that when I talk to parents."

In summary, the participants freely discussed the importance of Native educators to reservation schools. Two-thirds of the participants (including the majority of both affinitive and facilitative educators) went so far as to argue American Indian educators possess distinct advantages compared to non-Native educators. In their estimation, Native educators serve as important role models for students and parents are more likely to trust them. Some also identified the arrogant attitude of some non-Native educators as a barrier to their effectiveness. Given the unfortunate history of formal education for many tribal peoples, there are certainly compelling reasons to believe that Native educators enjoy advantages in reservation schools.

Research supports the perceptions of the educators regarding the advantages of American Indian educators. Among other benefits, previous research demonstrates that Native students are more likely to form positive relationships with American Indian teachers, and parents prefer and trust them (Chavers, 2000; Kawagley, 1999; Lipka & Mohatt, 1998; Miller Cleary & Peacock, 1998; Swisher & Tippeconnic, 1999). Furthermore, scholars have also documented how American Indian educators serve as important role models and provide greater connectivity to their communities (Cherubini, 2008; Manuelito, 2003; Miller Cleary & Peacock, 1998)

Even though most of the participants acknowledged the inherent advantages possessed by American Indian educators, they also understood the responsibilities that go along with being a Native teacher or principal on the reservation. They recognized the tremendous good American Indian teachers can provide and, ironically, the potential damage they can inflict on reservation children. Without offering much in the way of explanation, a Montana principal cautioned, "You always hear about an Indian educator can be more successful with an Indian student, but on the flip side an Indian educator can hurt an Indian student more than a white or non-Native teacher can." The sharp edge of serving as a role model cuts both ways.

Ways to Grow American Indian Educators

Given the need for American Indian educators, I wanted to learn how the participants believe reservations can grow greater numbers of American Indian teachers and administrators. A few of the participants candidly stated they did not know how reservations could increase the number of American Indian educators in their schools. One individual, a South Dakota teacher, altered the question slightly and addressed the issue of teacher retention. She concluded by simply saying she personally could not encourage individuals who had left the profession to return:

> There are a lot of Native teachers who start out and end up not surviving. . . . I can name five right off the bat that are right here in the reservation that are not in the classroom and are certified to teach. To me that's a waste. . . . To be honest, I wouldn't know how to pull them in. I wouldn't know what to say. I wouldn't know how to sell it because it is a lot of work. It is time consuming. You put a lot of yourself into it. You sit there and you see the kids who are having a hard time at home. It's stressful. You are so under the gun anymore.

This individual proved an exception among the participants. Most of the respondents appeared generally enthusiastic about their vocation and excited about the possibility of developing greater numbers of American Indian educators to serve reservation students. Unfortunately, they did not offer many suggestions for ways to increase the number of American Indian educators. The most frequent response offered by the participants involved using tribal colleges to prepare teachers for service in reservation schools. Twelve of the twenty-one participants believed teacher preparation programs at tribal colleges can facilitate larger numbers of American Indian educators. Six of the affinitive educators and six of the facilitative educators related that tribal college teacher preparation programs offer a reasonable and realistic way to provide the necessary training for Native educators. This view is not surprising, given the fact that more than half of the participants received training or degrees from local tribal colleges.

Not only did the participants identify tribal college teacher preparation programs as an important source of American Indian educators, but also several expressed a preference for teachers trained at tribal colleges over those, even American Indian educators, trained elsewhere. A South Dakota principal related that whenever a position opens at her school, she first contacts the local tribal college for possible new graduates. She said, "[They play] a big role [referring to the tribal college's assistance in providing the school's staffing needs]. Every year, if I knew somebody wasn't coming back, I would call the college and say, 'Do you have student teachers out there, anyone who is close to graduating?' So a lot of the teachers who are at [name of school] are graduates of the college. Probably half. And the master's program—a lot of our teachers go into their master's program."

Another educator, whose reservation does not have a tribal college equipped to prepare teachers, expressed her desire that reservations develop more teacher training programs. She explained tribal colleges are better suited to prepare educators to face the unique challenges of serving reservation schools: "I wish there was a program in tribal colleges that could grow their own and not necessarily in South Dakota State University or North Dakota State University, or whatever, because it is very different to want to teach in one of these schools. And not just the curriculum but the challenges that go along with classroom management. . . . I know there are tribal colleges that can do it [offer teacher education programs] that really know the problems we face and how you can become an educator and address those issues in schools."

While the participants generally demonstrated high esteem for tribal colleges as a potential source of future teachers, a couple of the educators did not share this view. Two of the educators were rather critical of the teacher preparation training provided by tribal colleges. For instance, regarding teachers trained at his local tribal college, one principal related,

Our superintendent has made it a priority to try and hire locals, people here. And they have done a good job of that. But it's also our job to try to get them to teach effectively and do the best they can in the classroom. That's kind of been a challenge for us. As we come in and we know what effective teaching is. . . . But to plan and come in and try to let them know, "Hey, this is what you need to do professionally. Plan effectively. If you make good lesson plans it will carry over in your classroom. Students are going to be more engaged, the attendance will probably go up because they will want to be in school. We are going to have less behavioral problems." So that's my biggest challenge right now as an administrator is to try and hold teachers accountable to be effective in the classroom. And I bet if you talked to everybody else on either a reservation or a BIE [Bureau of Indian Education] school I think that's probably our number one goal right now.

The majority of the participants also related that reservations can increase the number of American Indian educators by personally encouraging others to become teachers. It is the notion of "the strength of weak ties" whereby individuals working through personal networks can facilitate significant institutional change (Granovetter, 1973). Eleven of the twenty-one individuals stated they had encouraged others to consider education as a profession. Moreover, affinitive educators and facilitative educators reported comparable inclinations to personally recruit people to become teachers (six of the twelve affinitive educators and five of the nine facilitative educators).

One South Dakota teacher said she regularly encourages parents to become educators because that is how she made the decision to become a teacher herself. She reflected, "I myself talk to the parents. And they are so good at what they do because that is how I started. And I try to encourage them." However, the participants were more likely to report encouraging students rather than parents to consider a career in education. One South Dakota principal told me of his attempts to guide students into any postsecondary career, including education. Interestingly, this individual believed students, especially those who desire to become educators, should experience higher education off the reservation: "I'm always encouraging Native people to go beyond high school and go to postsecondary in whatever it is. I see some very bright students in our building and certainly I have talked to them about, 'Hey, maybe you should be an educator and come back and help your community.' I would like to see Natives take a leap and go beyond the reservation and experience a university [off the reservation] and I know that's culture shock because I've been through it."

A Montana principal described his attempts to encourage students to consider becoming teachers. Clearly, he recognized the importance of building self-confidence as part of guiding students to think about prospective career paths. Indeed, this individual's personal efforts had yielded impressive results. He related, "I see kids that work with other kids really well and I tell them I think they would be a good teacher. I tell them that they are a teacher whether they know it or not. And I'm seeing quite a few of them do that, actually. I can count at least six of my former students that are teachers now."

Several of the participants spoke of the need to offer specific guidance to students. These individuals understood many of their students must first overcome onerous obstacles before realizing any career goal. A South Dakota principal reflected on the situation:

> There are a lot of kids out there who have that potential. It's just having that support and leading them in the right direction and saying, "You can be successful. You can be a Native American educator and this is what you need to do." I think a lot of our kids don't understand that. And, like I said, being supportive, because these kids sometimes when they go home there is nothing to go home to. They are the adults in the family. They are the ones who have to deal with making sure their siblings are fed. But I do believe they can overcome that. We have kids who have overcome that and have gone on and have been successful. And we are starting to have more role models [American Indian educators] out there where kids might start taking a look and think, "I'd like to go into that."

A Montana principal believed that, while opportunities on the reservation exist for individuals to become teachers, many Native students need more than mere encouragement to enter the vocation. To him, educators must also address issues of self-confidence among their students:

> I think there is one thing that is easily overlooked that we don't do with the young people when we try to get them interested in becoming teachers. I think we don't instill the confidence in them because we're by nature sort of a humble, sort of quiet group of people. And I think what we could do more is instill in our kids the confidence to stand up and be a teacher. I think a lot of our people, they seem really quiet, really humble. I think that if in some ways we could build the confidence in them to stand up in front of classrooms and talk and teach.

Another Montana principal contended that, as parents gain a greater desire to become educators themselves, significant changes in attitudes toward education on the reservation will result. The first step includes getting parents involved in their children's education that, in his view, will lead to a greater understanding of the mission of schools, and will culminate in a desire to actively participate as a teacher. His comments suggest the intersection between encouraging others to become educators and dispelling negative perceptions about schools:

> To get them [parents] involved in their kids' lives I think is one thing. Because when parents come in here, and see that this is a positive place. This is where kids are learning, "Maybe I want to do that. Maybe I want to help kids." Doing this, I think, is one way to help to increase the number of Indian teachers, to dispel the myths about what school used to be like. This school, anyways, is not what it used to be like because I grew up in what it used to be like. I can remember getting a book cracked off your head, sticking your fingers out and getting a ruler across the fingers. I remember those days. I grew up in this same building. That's what it was like, and it's not that way anymore.

Certainly, the participants provided simple yet reasonable and realistic proposals on how reservations can produce more Native educators. Teacher preparation programs at local tribal colleges and personal encouragement of others to become educators represented the most prevalent approaches to increase the numbers of Native educators voiced by the participants. Their suggestions have great merit. The past three decades have witnessed the push to expand teacher preparation programs at tribal colleges, and several have emerged as major leaders in Native education training (Froelich & Medearis, 1999; Manuelito, 2003). Still, much more must be done in order to fill the needs of reservation schools (Beaulieu & Figueira, 2006; Swisher & Tippeconnic, 1999).

Significantly, the participants were also quick to point out that, while increasing the number of Native educators is important, other significant issues must be considered. Namely, the personal motivation and disposition of any potential educator goes a long way toward determining success in the classroom. Even those who identified tribal colleges as important sources for American Indian teachers caution that people need to see education as more than a convenient career choice. Simply put, people require a heart for teaching young people regardless of where they receive their teacher training. For the majority of these individuals, serving Native children must be regarded as a true vocational calling rather than merely an acceptable job option.

Cultural Strengths and Professional Efficacy

A rather fascinating finding involves how the cultural strengths of the participants enhance their professional efficacy. Seven of the twenty-one participants (three of the twelve affinitive and four of the nine facilitative educators) related they draw strength from their tribal culture. A Montana teacher discussed how the values and worldview he appropriates from his cultural heritage directly impacts his teaching practice. Particularly intriguing is that this individual mapped out the linkage between grounding in one's culture, pedagogical cultural relevancy and effectiveness, and his own professional aspirations to provide service to Native children:

> We got a story in our reading anthology about Sitting Bull's childhood and my kids love that. It's the only story about a Native American in their whole series, and it's their favorite one. They have to be exposed to other cultures and things like that but why can't we design a curriculum that's centered around their culture and their worldview and their shared experiences between all the tribes? . . . I think kids connect with that a lot. . . . And that should be a focal point. I would like to go and further my education and find out how I can be in a school system that makes that a focal point. How do we develop the curriculum? Get myself in a position to make those decisions in administration and do something along those lines.

A South Dakota teacher related her personal journey as an individual growing up in a culturally traditional family, leaving the reservation, and eventually returning as a teacher on her home reservation. During the interview, a variety of themes intersected, yet her focus centered on how grounding in tribal culture impacts her professional life. In this individual's estimation, her cultural identity equipped her for greater effectiveness as an educator:

> The identity is very important because you can really suffer as a Native American. It was real difficult leaving the reservation and going to a non-Native community and trying to get an education. Feeling the hardship of what it was to be Native. . . . It would become so discouraging living in a non-Native society and how it was at that point. . . . I guess that was a beautiful lesson for me. It was a hard teaching. But somewhere in there came a balance because I had seen my folks and grandparents being very Native and hanging in there. So it's a conditioning process as well having that Dakota way of life, being conditioned with traditions. Tradition and values are very important and they have really helped me in my life. . . . Our language is us. It is our identity. I know there is a difference, I don't know how to explain it, but I do know that as a speaker [of her tribal language] my thoughts are different than those of our people who

don't speak because they have pretty much lived in the dominant society where it is all non-Native speaking.

After we had discussed a number of other issues, I concluded our interview by giving her the last word to address any topic she desired. Interestingly, she returned to her personal journey and emphasized how her tribal cultural heritage and strength is foundational to her mission as an educator. She related how she attempts to develop those strengths in her students:

> I come from a strong background, being brought up in a real strong belief system and culture, a very diverse background. Being traditional but also because of survival being open to participate in non-Native churches. That is good if you can ground a lot of people that way. As an educator, you really need to get to know the student and appreciate their background. It's important to appreciate where they come from and try to facilitate understanding of the identity that they have because a lot of them don't even know what their identity is. So if you can facilitate that in that student then that is encouraging them to be the best they can be.

I did not initially ask about the connection between tribal culture and their work as educators, yet one-third of the participants volunteered that they draw on their cultural strengths as a way to enhance their professional efficacy. This finding is especially significant. It underscores the potential for tribal cultural identity and heritage to facilitate greater effectiveness in the classroom. Previous research demonstrates that Native educators frequently regard tribal cultural preservation as a primary reason for entering the profession (Begaye, 2007; Duquette, 2002). Obviously, they also must derive strength from their cultural heritage in much the same way as Native people engaged in mainstream cultural pursuits (White Shield, 2009).

An intriguing question remains: How do cultural strengths enhance professional efficacy? Unfortunately, the participants offered only partial insight into that question. Their comments suggest they derive a sense of purpose, identity, and direction in their professional lives from their personal cultural heritage. This is an area that requires further examination. As a result of this research, I plan to pursue deeper exploration into specifically how tribal cultural strengths impact the professional work of the educational practitioner.

COMPARISON OF AFFINITIVE EDUCATORS AND FACILITATIVE EDUCATORS

Affinitive educators and facilitative educators demonstrated few differences in their perspectives on the importance of American Indian educators or on ways reservations can develop greater numbers of tribal members to enter the profession. The only slight difference involves perceptions on tribal culture and their practice as professional educators. Facilitative educators were a little more likely to describe how grounding in tribal culture enhances their effectiveness as educators. Whereas a quarter of the affinitive educators (three out of the twelve) discussed the influence of tribal culture on their professional effectiveness, almost half of the facilitative educators did so (four of the nine).

This pattern is a little surprising because affinitive educators were more likely to describe early socialization experiences oriented toward traditional tribal culture. However, it is possible that, because of their cultural background, affinitive educators simply esteemed the integration of tribal values and beliefs as a normal part of their personal and professional worldview. They relate to students through the cultural experiences and styles that come naturally to them. For many of these individuals to reflect on the cultural perspective that frames their practice as educators would be much the same as reflecting on breathing—it is a natural part of what they do. Conversely, facilitative educators, who stressed the importance of professional effectiveness, were more likely to deliberate on the attributes that make an individual a good classroom teacher or building administrator. Consequently, many of them arrived at an awareness that grounding in tribal culture is essential to the effective education of Native children. Thus, a number of them specifically pointed out the importance of tribal culture in enhancing their practice as educators.

In essence, it may be that many of the facilitative educators were just beginning to truly discover and appropriate the cultural strengths of the tribe and use them in the classroom. Affinitive educators, by and large, viscerally understood cultural strengths and did not feel compelled to discuss their own grounding in tribal culture during the interviews. As will be shown in the next chapter, however, affinitive educators, like facilitative educators, had a great deal to say about the cultural identity of their students.

CONCLUSION

Like the participants in this study, a number of scholars argue that American Indian educators have distinct advantages over non-Native educators.

Specifically, local people are more likely to personally invest in the community, to understand the issues facing their own people, and to have greater legitimacy in dealing with parents and students, and are more likely to remain in their positions (Ambler, 2006; Boyer, 2006; Woodrum, 2009).

As the participants suggested, likely tribal colleges will assume an even larger role in supplying American Indian educators for reservation schools than they have in the past. Teacher preparation programs found in tribal colleges represent the most logical, viable, and reasonable source of American Indian educators (Cajete, 2006; Pavel et al., 2002). Moreover, it is logical to expect a number of important outcomes will result as greater numbers of American Indian educators emerge. These outcomes will most likely include higher graduation rates, more sweeping curricular changes to include richer and more meaningful elements of tribal culture, and positive alterations in community or school relations (Ambler, 2006; Boyer, 2006; Chavers, 2000; Grande, 2004; Klug & Whitfield, 2003; Miller Cleary & Peacock, 1998; Tippeconnic & Faircloth, 2006).

These are greatly optimistic projections, and simply having greater numbers of Native educators will not in itself guarantee a more effective educational system (Peshkin, 1997). Nevertheless, research suggests such outcomes are more likely to result if there are more Native educators than if there are fewer. In his research on American Indian high school dropouts in Montana, Theodore Coladarci (1983) found more than one-third of the participants believed their teachers did not care about them. Ultimately, personal relationships founded upon cultural understanding and appreciation may be as important as strong pedagogical practices and curriculum (Garrett, Bellon-Harn, Torres-Rivera, Garrett, & Roberts, 2003). Other researchers have found Native students frequently feel alienated by ineffective teaching practices and common stereotypes portraying them as less capable than non-Native students (Dingman, Mroczka, & Brady, 1995; Fox, 1999; Reyhner, 1992). Clearly, reservation schools require highly trained American Indian affinitive and facilitative educators. Tribal colleges can and likely should produce educators that have both these qualities (Lamb, 2010).

Currently many reservation schools have two functions: a manifest function to educate children and a latent function to help preserve tribal culture. However, as the twenty-first century progresses, that latent function is likely to become a pressing manifest one as a greater number of tribes enlist schools in the effort to preserve their cultures. If reservation schools are to achieve their fullest potential to both educate Native children and assist in cultural retention and preservation, they need greater numbers of culturally competent American Indian educators.

Certainly, the inherent advantages American Indian educators have in building interpersonal connections, delivering culturally relevant pedagogy, and engaging in effective teaching strategies are critically important issues. However, two additional interconnected issues loom large in the experiences of the American Indian educators I interviewed for this research. These matters are every bit as important as anything else discussed thus far because they relate to both the academic success of Native students and tribal cultural preservation. These two significant issues are the cultural identity of American Indian students and the nature of tribal cultural education in reservation schools. The next chapter explores the participants' perceptions and experiences on these compelling issues.

CHAPTER 7

You Have to Know the Culture
Cultural Identity and Tribal Cultural Education

> *I don't know for sure what happened. I really think we just didn't handle it right. You know they say in order to know the language you have to know the culture. So did we take the culture away in school settings?*
>
> —South Dakota educator lamenting tribal cultural loss and the lack of tribal cultural education in schools

Driving west across South Dakota making my way back home, the bright sun bore through the windshield so intensely that even with sunglasses I had to squint to see. It was impossible to miss the obvious cliché: with the research completed, I was literally riding off into the sunset. I had conducted the final interview just that morning and, filled with a sense of accomplishment, I reflected on my experiences, the people I had met, and all I had learned. More than any other feeling, I came away with tremendous respect and admiration for the individuals I had met. So many encounters, so many stories—they crowded my mind as the miles tracked behind me. As I drove into the darkness of a Wyoming night, one discussion in particular stood out.

The South Dakota principal had many years serving as an educator and was approaching retirement. She spoke her Native language fluently and embraced the traditions of her people. She also was a highly respected and noted educator. If anyone had the vantage point of years of professional experience and tribal cultural knowledge, certainly she did. With the wisdom of a school leader and a tribal elder, she talked about the current state of affairs on her reservation:

> I just talked to a man who works in the Tribal Education office about the culture and how we can have families learn the language. And he was talking about the barriers on the reservation of the importance of the language. They surveyed people in the community and they don't feel like they need to know the language. "Why would I want

to know it?," "It's not going to help me get a job," "No one to talk to." We have a lot of work to do if that's the thought in the community. And I was sharing with him that when I taught Head Start years ago, [name of community] was probably the most traditional community and hardly any of those kids are speaking the language anymore down there. And it hasn't been boarding schools or anything like that that has taken it away. It's just like, what happened? We would pick those kids up, little four year olds, and they'd just be speaking the language. And no one ever said you can't speak it. It was allowed. And there was some teachers who could speak the language too who could speak to them. . . . It is sad to think that people don't think it's important to know the language.

When I embarked on this research journey I knew I wanted to explore a variety of significant issues and the preceding chapters have related much of what I discovered about the roles the educators see themselves performing, the intrinsic rewards as well as prevailing challenges they encounter, their experiences of teaching in reservation schools during the era of NCLB, and their thoughts on the importance of American Indian educators to reservation schools and communities. This final chapter, however, is different from the previous ones. In this chapter, I focus on two specific and related issues while simultaneously engaging in theoretical reflection and consideration. Specifically, I apply transculturation theory as a way to examine the participants' perceptions on their students' cultural identity and the nature of tribal cultural education.

Transculturation theory contends a strong cultural identity is essential for academic success for American Indian students (see appendix for details). Using this theoretical perspective as a guide, I analyzed the responses of the educators in order to first consider their perceptions on the cultural identity of students, and second to consider their views on the nature of the tribal cultural education offered in their schools. As I explained in chapter 5, by "tribal cultural education" I mean culturally relevant curriculum and instruction as well as the infusion of tribal values and worldview. There is a direct connection between the cultural identity of students and the way schools deliver tribal cultural education. Simply put, if educators regard strong cultural identity as critically important to the personal, social, emotional, and academic development of students, then they place high value on tribal cultural education.

In the first chapter, I introduced the five basic research questions that framed my research on American Indian educators serving reservation students. In this chapter, I also recap the major findings on those research questions. Finally, I discuss some of the theoretical and applied implications associated with the findings.

TRANSCULTURATION THEORY, CULTURAL IDENTITY, AND TRIBAL CULTURAL EDUCATION

Scholars use transculturation theory primarily to examine the experiences of American Indian college students. However, I reasoned that transculturation theory also could aid in understanding the experiences and perceptions of educational professionals who teach with one foot in the mainstream (e.g., schools largely based on mainstream standards and curriculum) and one foot in more culturally traditional settings (e.g., reservation communities). Transculturation theory rests on the fundamental assertion that a strong cultural identity promotes effective participation in mainstream institutions. Operating from this premise, I wanted to examine if the participants would identify a strong cultural identity as essential for the academic and personal success of their students and whether they would regard schools as instruments to reinforce tribal culture. Thus, I created a working hypothesis both to guide the questions I asked of the participants as well as to guide what I was looking for during the analysis of the data: *The participants will emphasize the importance of a strong cultural identity among their students and the need for tribal cultural education to support the cultural identity development of students.*

I intentionally did not include questions directly addressing my working hypothesis on the interview schedule. For instance, I did not ask, "Is it important for students to possess a strong cultural identity?" While that question addresses the working hypothesis, it is obviously leading and sure to generate specific responses. Who would answer "no" to such a question? Instead, I offered a global question (and occasional probes) that allowed the educator to answer in whatever fashion he or she wished. Specifically, I asked the respondents, "Let's talk about tribal culture and language and schools. What issues, thoughts, and experiences would you like to tell me about regarding tribal culture and the education of Native students?" I reasoned that by presenting such an open-ended question the participants would answer in the manner most significant to their experiences as educators. Furthermore, I had confidence in the strength of transculturation theory's assertion that a strong cultural identity is critical for American Indian students, and I believed the participants would likely gravitate toward this issue in their responses. Conversely, if the participants did not indicate these views or if they provided answers contradictory to the key assumption of transculturation theory, then the data analysis would reveal that cultural identity may not be as essential in the estimation of these participants as the theory proposes.

Cultural Identity Issues

The data analysis revealed two findings associated with cultural identity issues. A number of the educators believed many Native students suffer cultural ambiguity and require a strong cultural identity, and almost an equal number related that a strong cultural identity facilitates academic and life success.

Generally, the educators I met recognized the importance of a strong cultural identity for their students. Indeed, eleven of the twenty-one individuals expressed concern over what they considered the cultural identity ambiguity experienced by their students. Namely, they believed that many Native students do not highly regard their own ethnicity or attempt to appropriate the cultural identity of other ethnic groups. The lack of a strong cultural identity creates confusion and uncertainty for these students. Furthermore, there was no difference among the affinitive and facilitative educators on this perception. Seven of the twelve affinitive educators and four of the nine facilitative educators discussed the cultural identity difficulties of their students. Typical is a Montana principal who described his students as being lost because they do not have a tribal point of reference to anchor their lives:

> I think our kids are lost in some ways. They're searching for some kind of spiritual, higher calling and they're searching for their identity, they're searching for their culture, they're searching for anything they can latch on to, and it's just not there. In some ways, you are just a [name of tribe] and not really connected to your culture. . . . Because our kids don't speak much language, they don't have any sort of spiritual base to their traditional culture. They really don't know a whole lot about it.

Several of the educators described how American Indian youth attempt to find replacement cultures to compensate for personal cultural ambiguity. For example, a South Dakota middle school teacher explained, "A lot of our young people are looking for their identities in everything else, like in the music. There is either African American music or there's all these different types of rap music and all these influences from the media. It's a different way of life. It's a real challenge."

Two of the participants described the rejection of tribal culture among students. One, a Montana principal, contended educators can combat the cultural rejection displayed by young people by stressing the importance of tribal culture:

> At times it is even to where the kids are totally against it. Kind of rejecting their Native roots. . . . I think part of the reason why kids are tagging things and part of the reason why they are getting into gangs is they have this idea that to be Native is bad. They get it from all over. I know that one of the things we have tried to do here is to say, "No, we are pretty proud of who we are and it's time we need to clean this up and we need to do this because that is who we are." . . . Just emphasizing the part that it's okay to be Native American. We don't have to listen to what the media says or we don't have to fall into the stereotypes, we don't have to do any of that other stuff. We just have to be who we are. And that's okay.

The other participant, a South Dakota elementary teacher, expressed concern over the deep-seated cultural rejection she has witnessed in some of her students. In a poignant story, she related a revealing encounter with a former student:

> It is their identity. It's who they are. There was a young man one time and he came to the house and he was drinking. And he said, "Can I talk to you?" He was one of the students I knew and he was older now. He said, "I'm ashamed to be Indian." And I said, "Why? Why are you ashamed to be Indian?" "Because," he said, "they always talk about us being dog eaters and make fun of us being poor and living on the welfare system and being dumb." . . . When I talked to that boy I told him, "I do not know what it is like to be ashamed to be Indian. I know what it is like when people make you feel bad and say things about Indian people that you know aren't true. That's out of ignorance. They don't know who you are. There is a lot of good things about you. We give to the people. People don't understand that." It made me really feel bad because there are a lot of kids out there like that. So it's really important [to establish a strong cultural identity] because then they can succeed and make a decision to say, "Okay, I know who I am." They are not lost, trying to figure out that part of it.

A Montana principal described her efforts to enhance the cultural self-identity of third grade students. One can easily gather that her effectiveness with small children emerges from the strength of her own cultural identity:

> "Have you ever seen a real Indian?" I asked that question of my third graders the last year I was teaching. I said, "Raise your hand if any of you have ever seen a real Indian." Every single one of those kids was Indian, by the way. Three hands went up—three

hands went up! And one kid raised his hand and he said, "Wait, now, I think I did. Well, my uncle did." [Laughs.] And I had a little mirror and I walked around and showed them it. I said, "When you're looking in this mirror, you're looking at a real Indian. I said, when you look at me, you're looking at a real Indian. And being Indian doesn't mean having powwow regalia, it's who we are." And so I worked all year long to instill that in them. And so at the end of the year, I said, "Raise your hand if you ever seen a real Indian." And all their hands went up. "We see one every time we look in the mirror."

Almost half of the participants, ten of the twenty-one, believed grounding in tribal culture facilitates academic and personal success. Once again affinitive educators and facilitative educations demonstrate similar patterns in their responses on this issue. Five of the twelve affinitive educators and five of the nine facilitative educators indicated cultural grounding leads to academic and life success. This perception is, of course, consistent with transculturation theory's assertion that a strong cultural identity equips Native students with the means to succeed. A Montana educator explained why he believes tribal cultural grounding facilitates success among Native students:

If you are taught your cultural values and your cultural history, I think we would see a lot more success in Indian communities educationally. Because you can teach the reading skills and the writing skills through just about any point of view, but I think in an Indian community there is a unique point of view. Oftentimes that perspective is neglected by our education system and I think the kids would connect with it and connect with school a lot more if it was taught in a way that matched their worldview. . . . I would like to see some more traditional values stressed in our school days and these kids understand that's it about community. It's about the people. You trace back Native names [of tribal groups] and translate those names, and they translate into like, "the First People," or "the Real People." That's their identity before they are individuals. They are part of something that's greater than themselves.

Another Montana teacher related a similar perspective. In fact, his experiences are consistent with transculturation theory's assertion that culturally oriented American Indian students succeed academically and in life because they draw strength from their culture and identity:

There is more than a few that do speak their language and they follow their culture. But they come from solid backgrounds where they have grandparents who are in the home or they have access to grandparents. Their families are culturally orientated. They speak the language at home. Those are the kids that succeed. Because right now we are almost like at a crossroad in our culture here. You can almost identify the kids that are going to succeed in life. . . . And those are the types of kids I see that are succeeding, that have a strong background in their culture and their language . . . And it comes from their parents. Their parents have to believe that education is the path to success. And it's both sides. It's got to be our traditions and our cultural knowledge combined with educational knowledge. If you are armed with those two, you have your spear in one hand and you have your pipe and shield in the other hand, and you walk down that road of education, I think you are going to succeed.

Tribal Cultural Education Issues

I found intriguing the views of the participants on tribal cultural education as emphasized (or not emphasized) in their schools. Because I was working from the transculturation theoretical framework that holds a cultural foundation as critical for academic success, I was attentive to their perceptions and experiences around this issue. At the outset of the investigation, I assumed the educators would likely discuss issues directly connected to the cultural identity development needs of students. However, the respondents went beyond this issue and described ways in which reservation schools support not only their students' cultural needs, but also those of the larger tribe. Based on the accounts offered by the participants, tribal cultural education in reservation schools is filled with potential, complexities, and no small amount of frustration. They generally believed schools can provide tremendous service by helping to enhance or even preserve tribal cultural traditions and language. A number of them also were frustrated over the lack of leadership and commitment to tribal cultural education.

The analysis of the interviews revealed three themes associated with tribal cultural education. First, the participants regarded general culturally relevant pedagogical practices as well as specific tribal cultural curriculums as vitally important components of the education of Native children. Second, they said schools can assist in the preservation of tribal culture and language. Third, a number of the participants conveyed their frustration with the lack of leadership required to guide tribal cultural education efforts.

Sixteen of the twenty-one educators discussed the importance of culturally relevant teaching practices and learning experiences for American Indian children. I found virtually no difference between affinitive educators and facilitative educators on this issue. Nine of the twelve affinitive educators and seven of the nine facilitative educators discussed the necessity for culturally appropriate and relevant classroom approaches and tribal cultural curriculum. A

South Dakota educator spoke of the natural and simple ways in which the educators at his school make learning experiences culturally relevant for students. His comments are illustrative of the views typically expressed by the participants: "It's important that we connect the culture with what we are doing in the classroom. And I've been in classrooms where they will talk about the Native traditions versus historical implications. And it's a really effective lesson if you can connect that because it's meaningful for our students. I think they get a lot more out of that lesson if you connect that culture piece."

Other educators spoke of the need for curriculum specially designed to teach tribal history, language, and traditions. A Montana teacher related his efforts to infuse tribal history and traditions when teaching young students: "We do a lot of discussion and we talk about how there is a textbook history and I tell my kids there is a history that is for the most part unwritten for elementary kids. So I try to bring as much of that perspective from my Native American studies background as I can to my social studies curriculum."

Most of the educators expressed great concern over the loss of tribal culture and language. Additionally, a majority of the participants believed reservation schools can serve their communities by assisting to preserve tribal cultural history, language, and traditions. In fact, fifteen of the twenty-one educators contended schools can and should be instruments of cultural preservation. Again, I found little difference in the perceptions held by affinitive educators (eight of the twelve) and facilitative educators (seven of the nine).

A Montana educator reflected on the potential for schools to help preserve the tribal history and language of his people. He compared his own personal educational experiences as a student growing up on the reservation with the potential for schools to provide cultural learning experiences for students:

> In a lot of tribes, traditional culture is being replaced by the mainstream culture. One of the places where traditional culture, values, and behavior can be preserved is in our schools. We need like-minded educators who think along those lines and want to preserve tribal identity and tribal history so those kids can have a connection to their past and understand who they are and where they come from and why they are in a situation that they are in. Why do they live on a reservation? When we went to school, we weren't taught that. We were not taught tribal history. We were given the textbook history and it was hard to connect to it because it wasn't ours.

A South Dakota teacher explained schools must play a critical role in preserving tribal culture because frequently pressing personal and family challenges occupy the immediate attention of parents, so reservation schools must stand in the breach of cultural loss:

> They [students] all have that beautiful background. They come from that heritage. So once you start talking with them about where they come from or the importance of what that value is, that cultural value of generosity, of humility, you are attaching the language and the meaning and how one carries himself. . . . So much of that has been put on the back burner. . . . So a lot of that is missing from their lives and they don't even know it. That's a lot of it because we have oppression and depression. We've got high unemployment. Many times our families at home aren't going to be able to say, "We come from a beautiful history. We come from a beautiful culture." They're trying to figure out how to pay bills. They're trying to figure out how to put food on the table. So somewhere like here at [name of the school] we can provide culture and history and the beautiful things that we really come from and the sacrifices of the ancestors.

While the educators recognized the potential for schools to assist in cultural preservation, a few also contended reservation schools fail to prepare students with necessary tribal cultural education. For a Montana educator, the combination of a lack of resources in the school district and the declining number of individuals fluent in her language pose serious threats not only to the potential for reservation schools to assist with cultural preservation, but also to the cultural integrity of the tribe. She lamented, "I really fear for my people here because our language teacher in the school has retired and the people that speak the language, they're getting older, and they're dying. So it's like, okay, who's going to carry that on when they're gone? It's scary because our whole culture is in that language."

Some of the participants indicated frustration with the lack of leadership either in their district specifically or on the reservation generally in regards to tribal cultural education. Seven of the twenty-one participants expressed the need for greater visionary and effective leadership before schools can fulfill their cultural responsibilities to students and the community. Affinitive educators (five of the twelve) were more likely to mention this concern than were facilitative educators (two of the nine). Additionally, of the seven individuals who specifically discussed the lack of leadership on tribal cultural education in schools, six were from South Dakota and only one was from Montana. As mentioned in chapter 5, Montana's Indian Education for All initiative requires that educators infuse American Indian history and culture into the curriculum. It is possible this initiative impacts the Montana educators' perceptions on the leadership associated with American Indian education.

Indeed, a South Dakota educator put the matter rather bluntly: "It's frustrating for us because that's part of the district's founding documents that we are going to respect the culture and language. But the district doesn't do a very good job walking the talk."

A South Dakota educator candidly discussed her frustration with the lack of leadership on tribal cultural education. For this individual, a general failure among classroom teachers and administrators has resulted in terrible consequences:

> For so long the tribe depended on the schools to teach it and it didn't happen. We have kids in the high school and middle school who can beat other schools in the [American Indian tribe] Language Bowl but it is just a competition. It's not to speak the language every day. I would like to bring in the culture a lot more. And I think the more they hear the language and the importance of it, there might be people who say, "I want to go further and learn the language." Because we are really losing our students fast. Because we have lost that [traditional culture] I think they are looking elsewhere to replace it and we have so many gangs and the suicide rate is so high, and the hopelessness. It is a big challenge because it's not just a school challenge. It's a reservation-wide challenge.

COMPARISON OF AFFINITIVE EDUCATORS AND FACILITATIVE EDUCATORS

Affinitive educators and facilitative educators displayed some of the closest agreement on the topics covered in this chapter. The two types of educators evidenced remarkably similar patterns in their responses regarding concerns over the cultural identity of students and nature of tribal cultural education in reservation schools. Only on one perception did affinitive educators and facilitative educators seem to diverge—frustration over leadership and tribal cultural education. Five of the twelve affinitive educators voiced uneasiness regarding the leadership required to provide tribal cultural education compared to only two of the nine facilitative educators. Perhaps because affinitive educators are more likely to come from traditionally oriented backgrounds they displayed greater apprehension over what they regarded as a lack of urgency to respond to cultural loss among the local leadership. On the other hand, because facilitative educators take a more instrumental approach to their profession, they may have been more likely to look for leadership and solutions within their school system than to rely on leadership external to the school system.

With that being said, a more significant factor may be the differing professional experiences between Montana educators and South Dakota educators than any difference between affinitive and facilitative educators. Again, it is important to note that of the seven participants who specifically voiced frustration over a lack of effective leadership to guide tribal cultural education, six were from South Dakota. Possibly Montana's Indian Education for All initiative has significantly contributed to the difference in the experiences and perceptions displayed by the Montana educators and the South Dakota educators. Montana educators could point to tangible support provided by the state's political and education leadership that the South Dakota educators simply did not have.

EVALUATION OF TRANSCULTURATION THEORY

The educators who participated in this research generally regarded a strong cultural identity reinforced by culturally relevant pedagogy and curriculum as important to the success of students. Their experiences reveal the need for a secure cultural foundation among students. Moreover, they also believed schools can provide cultural grounding for students while simultaneously serving the reservation by assisting to preserve tribal traditions and language. Their perceptions align with the assertions found within transculturation theory. Indeed, many of the participants addressed issues of cultural identity and tribal education presented to them in open-ended questioning in the manner indicated by this theoretical framework. This, of course, does not provide empirical evidence that students with a strong cultural identity reinforced by tribal education are more academically successful, but it does demonstrate that a substantial proportion of the American Indian educators in this study believed that to be the case.

While this investigation did not empirically test the validity of the perceptions offered by the participants, a number of researchers have documented findings supporting their views. Research over the past twenty years provides evidence for the importance of a strong cultural identity among Native students. Robert Vadas (1995) reported a connection between identification with Native language, culture, and traditions, with a number of positive educational outcomes among a sample of Navajo middle and high school students. Although his findings on the relationship between adherence to tribal traditions and academic achievement are mixed, Vadas concludes that a strong cultural identity enhances the self-esteem and sense of personal purpose among Native students. These attributes are obviously related to academic achievement.

Whitbeck, Hoyt, Stubben, and LaFromboise (2001) explored a variety of factors associated with educational success among nearly 200 American Indian children from three reservations located in the Upper Plains. They found identification with traditional culture positively related to success in school. In a similar study, using survey research with 240 urban American Indian students, Powers (2006), too, found an important link between positive educational outcomes and cultural identity. She examined the relationship between culturally based educational practices, including efforts to affirm the cultural identity and heritage of Native students with academic results. Powers reported culture-based educational programs are associated with the perception of a safe, secure school environment, greater parental involvement, and the perception of instructional quality.

In contrast to the findings reported in these studies, Rumbaugh Whitesell, Mitchell, and Spicer (2009) did not find a significant relationship between cultural identity and academic success in a longitudinal study with more than 1,600 American Indian students. These authors suggest that "students with high American Indian identity might actually reject academic goals as not consistent with traditional American Indian ways" (p. 39). However, the findings reported by Rumbaugh Whitesell and colleagues may not be as contradictory to the general conclusions reached by other researchers as they might appear. Likely both assertions are correct. That is, many Native students need a strong identity to succeed in schools but some students with a strong cultural identity reject schools as foreign institutions that do not represent their cultural values, worldview, and identity (Peshkin, 1997). Indeed, I found culturally oriented college students diverge largely in the way they use their cultural identity (Huffman, 2001, 2008). Specifically, one group holding a strong culturally oriented identity rejected the university as representing mainstream values and worldview, and dropped out. Another group used their strong culturally oriented identity as an emotional and cultural anchor to proceed through and eventually succeed in college. A similar situation likely exists among precollege students enrolled in reservation schools as occurs among postsecondary students attending largely non-Native universities and colleges. Indeed, many of the educators articulated experiences similar to the Montana educator mentioned in chapter 1 who described what he referred to as a "reverse racism mentality." This mindset leads some students to dismiss academic success as being "only for white students." Nevertheless, the educators also recognized other Native students use their cultural identity to confidently proceed through school.

A strong cultural identity may be essential for American Indian educational success, but of equal importance is the guidance offered by Native educators. As Miller Cleary and Peacock (1998) succinctly argue, "Schools that acknowledge, accept, and teach a child's cultural heritage have significantly better success in educating these students" (p. 108). Brown, Gibbons, and Eretzian Smirles (2007) documented the importance of tribal teachers in guiding the cultural identity development of adolescents. Although they did not specifically identify reservation school educators as tribal teachers, their findings are nonetheless relevant to the potential role schools may perform in this regard. They conclude that one of the most powerful factors in developing a tribal identity for adolescents is the number of adult tribal teachers from which to learn. Outside of families (and the mass media), young children and adolescents are unlikely to have greater persistent exposure to learning experiences than they have in schools. Brown and colleagues' findings reinforce the potential for reservation Native educators to provide tribal education to students and, thereby, to assist in efforts to preserve the culture.

The findings from my research provide tentative evidence that scholars can make wider use of transculturation theory to explain phenomena beyond the higher educational experiences of American Indian college students. The theory proved useful in directing inquiry into the perceptions on the cultural identity issues held by the American Indian educators in this study. It supplied a framework to explore issues of theoretical and applied importance while also equipping me with the essential concept to explain the experiences and perceptions articulated by the participants. In that regard, transculturation theory demonstrated its merits as a theoretical perspective. Just as important, transculturation theory allows scholars to understand issues of cultural identity strength and academic issues without relying on assimilationist-based explanations found in past scholarship (Huffman, 2005, 2010; Pewewardy, 2002; Scott, 1986).

RETRACING STEPS

As outlined in the Introduction, at the beginning of the investigation I posed five research questions. These questions served to give the project structure and direction; the preceding chapters outlined the general findings for each question. It is a good time now to revisit those research questions and summarize the answers.

Research Question #1: How do the participants describe their roles as American Indian educators serving reservation students and communities?

The roles performed by the participants are complex and multidimensional. They did not play a single role, but rather a variety of functions depending on specific circumstances and needs. The participants separated into two groups based on how they described their roles as American Indian educators. I treated these two groups as a typology consisting of affinitive educators and facilitative educators. Both shared deep concern and commitment to reservation students, schools, and communities, but they differed in the kinds of roles they emphasized and articulated. Affinitive educators described their primary responsibilities as serving as a role model and creating personal relationships with their students. Facilitative educators stressed the instrumental benefits of education and worked hard to be as effective and professionally competent as possible.

While this typology is offered as a conceptual framework intended to help us understand how the participants in this research regarded and interpreted their roles, I also believe it has usefulness beyond this study. That is, this typology provides scholars and educational practitioners alike with a way to systematically consider the professional practice of reservation educators. American Indian children have many needs—educational, social, emotional, and cultural. Children require teachers who have both affinitive and facilitative qualities: one overly dominant set of personality traits will not suffice. Too much emphasis on the attributes common to one side or the other of the typology would be a disservice to Native students. Teacher preparation programs must be deliberate in how they train educators for reservation classrooms by recognizing the strengths of both affinitive educators and facilitative educators and by instructing future educators to adopt a balance between the characteristics of each.

Research Question #2: What do the participants identify as their most compelling intrinsic rewards and challenges in serving reservation students and communities?

Unfortunately, I cannot provide a simple answer to this research question. Like the roles the participants regarded as most important, the rewards and challenges are too complex for one straightforward answer. Persistent difficulties with reservation social conditions, general attitudes toward education, diverse student-related issues, as well as school staff issues vexed the participants. The most common problems—that is, those identified by at least half of the twenty-one educators—include poverty (sixteen), family dysfunctions (fourteen), community indifference toward education (thirteen), lack of family support for education (twelve), and discipline problems (eleven). Conversely, the most common rewards identified by at least half of the participants include witnessing the success of students (sixteen) and awareness that they make a difference in students' lives (sixteen).

Frankly, the participants identified a lot more challenges than rewards and spent a greater amount of time discussing the challenges they face than the rewards they accrue. That does not mean the challenges outweigh the rewards, however. In fact, I found just the opposite to be the case. The educators displayed inspiring commitment and optimism. Indeed, almost all the participants told me the intrinsic rewards surpass the challenges.

Research Question #3: Is there a relationship between the roles the participants describe and the intrinsic rewards and challenges they identify?

The findings provide some intriguing insights into how the participants defined their roles and the kinds of intrinsic rewards and challenges they identified. Generally, affinitive educators and facilitative educators shared a number of similar challenges. However, many of these challenges have a specific nature to them. Namely, they are the kinds of issues that pervasively impact reservation life; all educators, no matter how they perceive their roles, cannot escape them. I refer to these difficulties as core challenges. Yet, there are a smaller number of issues that appear to be associated with how affinitive educators and facilitative educators perceived and defined their specific roles. Affinitive educators were more likely than facilitative educators to identify as challenges community scrutiny on American Indian educators, disregard for American Indian educators, and prejudicial attitudes among some non-Native educators. Facilitative educators were more prone to describe challenges related to discipline problems and ineffective peers. I refer to these challenges as peripheral challenges because they are more idiosyncratic to the way affinitive and facilitative educators define their roles.

A similar pattern emerged in regards to the intrinsic rewards the participants described. I identified two types of rewards—affirming rewards and altruistic rewards. Affirming rewards confirm and validate the work of the educator and typically derive from either witnessing the achievements of students or from receiving the gratitude expressed by others. Thus, these rewards tend to be essentially external to the individual. Altruistic rewards result from the satisfaction gained in knowing one has helped others or contributed to the betterment of the reservation community; they result from the intuitive, internal awareness of the individual. While affinitive educators and facilitative educators found most rewarding sharing in the success of students (an affirming reward) and the gratification of making a difference in students' lives (an altruistic reward), they demonstrated some differences on other rewards. Affinitive educators were slightly more likely to describe affirming rewards (expressions of appreciation presented by others) while facilitative educators were more inclined to discuss altruistic rewards (awareness of helping the reservation and assisting to preserve tribal culture). It does appear that the way the participants in this study defined their roles as educators is associated with many of the intrinsic rewards they identify as most important. To put it another way, affinitive educators and facilitative educators appeared to be sensitive to slightly different forms of intrinsic rewards. Namely, affinitive educators were a little more likely to describe affirming rewards whereas facilitative educators were slightly more inclined to describe altruistic rewards.

Research Question #4: How do the participants regard the impact of No Child Left Behind, especially its emphasis on standardized testing, on their students and schools?

A significant portion of the participants in this study reported frustration, pressure, and resentment over many of the mandates associated with NCLB. More than half of the educators regarded standardized tests in general and those specifically required by NCLB as inappropriate assessment tools. They deemed these tests to be incapable of measuring the true abilities of the American Indian students in their schools. A third of the participants believed the emphasis on standardized testing in the core content areas of math and reading as mandated by NCLB has diminished efforts to provide tribal cultural education. Only three educators stated that NCLB has not harmed tribal cultural education efforts. Additionally, one-third of the participants described feeling pressure in attempting to achieve adequate yearly progress, the measure of proficiency established under NCLB mandates. Indeed, none of the nine schools I visited for this research was making NCLB and, therefore, all were under threat of sanctions.

Affinitive educators and facilitative educators evidenced a remarkable difference on all of these issues. In every instance, affinitive educators were more likely than facilitative educators to express concern and distress over standardized tests, NCLB, and achieving AYP. For instance, while two-thirds of the affinitive educators believed standardized tests represent an inappropriate method to measure the proficiency of Native children, nearly half of the facilitative educators esteemed standardized tests as appropriate assessment devices. The difference in their respective experiences and perceptions is likely due to the way affinitive educators and facilitative educators defined their roles as educators; these definitions, at least in part, result from their respective cultural backgrounds. Affinitive educators who frequently described culturally oriented family backgrounds tended to emphasize the importance of personal relationships. As a result, they were less prone to embrace the highly structured, formalized assessment procedures associated with NCLB and AYP. Conversely, facilitative educators, who less frequently described culturally oriented family backgrounds, tended to stress the need to be effective classroom teachers and building administrators. Most facilitative educators were the products of traditional teacher training programs as undergraduate students or came to a career in education via a direct path, and so were perhaps more familiar and comfortable with the kinds of formal assessments and procedures typically associated with NCLB.

Research Question #5: Will the participants report they recognize the need to build the cultural identity of their students as suggested by transculturation theory?

The findings clearly demonstrate the educators appreciated the importance of a strong cultural identity for their students. More than half of the participants related that their students suffer from cultural ambiguity and need a strong cultural identity. Additionally, almost half of the educators believed a strong cultural identity facilitates academic success. These perceptions and experiences are consistent with the fundamental premise of transculturation theory.

Connected to the cultural identity needs of American Indian students, the participants also contended reservation schools require tribal cultural education in the form of culturally relevant pedagogy and tribal cultural education curriculum. Furthermore, they believed schools can serve their tribes by helping to preserve tribal culture and language. Unfortunately, a third of the participants indicated frustration with the lack of political and school leadership to guide tribal cultural education.

The general findings indicate the utility of transculturation theory as an explanative framework. They suggest the potential use of this theoretical perspective to understand the cultural identity issues of reservation schoolchildren and the nature of tribal cultural education. In short, transculturation theory is useful to account for phenomena beyond American Indian higher education and may emerge as a primary theoretical perspective in American Indian education studies.

LESSONS LEARNED

In this book I have presented the perceptions and experiences of twenty-one American Indian educational professionals. It is important to bear in mind those perceptions are more than idiosyncratic impressions: they represent experiences born from years of service to reservation students, schools, and communities. We can derive a number of important theoretical and applied implications from their professional and personal experiences.

The notion of transculturation served as a sensitizing concept guiding this research. The findings offer preliminary support for transculturation theory as a tool in understanding phenomena beyond the postsecondary experiences of American Indian students. Namely, the participants in this study generally indicated experiences and perceptions consistent with transculturation theory's fundamental premise that a strong cultural identity facilitates educational success, especially for culturally oriented Native students. Closer examination of the issues and barriers associated with the cultural identity development of American Indians enrolled in reservation schools using transculturation theory promises important avenues for future research. More specifically, researchers need to examine the cultural identity issues from the personal perspective of the students themselves. Qualitative research exploring how American Indian adolescents perceive, value, and utilize their cultural identity offers enormous promise both as applied and as pure scholarship. Such efforts would provide insights important to practitioners directly involved in the education of Native children and would add to the growing scholarship on transculturation theory.

The participants in this study contended a strong cultural identity facilitates academic and life success. Scholars need to undertake additional work on the relationship between cultural identity and academic achievement and personal lifestyle choices among precollege students. Certainly some work has been done in this area already (see Powers, 2006; and Whitbeck et al., 2001). However, these researchers did not operate specifically from transculturation theory. While more qualitative scholarship is required to build and expand the assumptions of this theoretical framework, greater quantitative research is also needed to systematically and empirically test the fundamental premise that a strong cultural identity is associated with academic achievement as predicted by transculturation theory.

Researchers should also explore the cultural identity of American Indian educators. A number of the participants indicate grounding in tribal culture enhances their professional efficacy as educators. Research on transculturated teachers (individuals conversant with both tribal and mainstream cultures) serving in reservation classrooms would be nothing short of fascinating.

The findings also suggest significant political and educational policy implications. Generally, the educators I interviewed realized the vital importance of culturally relevant educational practices. Other scholars have documented valuable ways in which Native and non-Native teachers can develop and deliver culturally relevant instruction (Miller Cleary & Peacock, 1998; Zehr, 2007). Many of the participants in this study suggested that they use something more than deliberately crafted classroom practices, however. They related that American Indian educators need to infuse tribal values, worldview, and language in substantial ways into instruction. This goes well beyond simply using a few cultural elements as add-ons to current instructional practices: it suggests a natural integration of tribal culture delivered by teachers who truly understand tribal values and worldview (Skinner, 1999). This proposes the need for transculturated American Indian teachers who effectively operate within the cultural mainstream but who are equally conversant with the worldview and values of their tribe.

If pedagogy is how teachers teach, then curriculum constitutes what they teach. Reservation tribal leaders must encourage and support their school leaders to develop tribal cultural education curriculums specific to their people's needs. However, policy and educational leaders need to recognize that when it comes to cultural education, one size does not fit all. An "American Indian" cultural education curriculum is not as good as a "tribal" cultural education curriculum. Tribes have a shared history they can and should draw from, certainly, but the unique features of each tribe's history, traditions, and language should not be ignored for a generic American Indian curriculum. Certainly, this will present numerous challenges and require great resources, especially for the many reservations populated by more than one tribal peoples. Nevertheless, the potential benefits derived from such curricular developments are likely inestimable in terms of student success, the development of reservation communities, and cultural retention.

The findings reveal the need for tribal leaders to recruit highly qualified American Indian educators who are conversant with good teaching practices, subject content, and tribal culture. Likely tribal colleges will continue to play a crucial role in these efforts. It only makes sense that tribal colleges are better situated to equip educators to meet the unique social, cultural, and pedagogical needs of reservation children (Ambler, 1999; Boyer 2006). The expansion or creation of teacher education programs at tribal colleges should be a top priority for tribal government leaders and tribal college leaders. Furthermore, the recruitment of quality individuals into these programs will be required. Beesley, Atwill, Blair, and Barley (2010) refer to the recruitment of local residents as educators as a "grow your own" strategy for rural schools. Such recruitment efforts will likely require targeted incentives such as tuition waivers, stipends while in school, and access to continued professional development (Beesley et al., 2010).

Finally, the findings reveal that the participants recognized reservation schools can and should be a mechanism to help preserve tribal culture. The greater enlistment of schools to assist in cultural preservation will require nothing less than a monumental shift in thinking and decision making. The participants frequently pointed to the persistent indifference toward education on their reservations. Many indicated their tribal leadership was apathetic toward schools and their mission. A Montana teacher eloquently summarized his frustration with the lack of leadership on education and pointed to the implications of continued diffidence:

> Community leaders, tribal governments need to stress that [the importance of schools].... But if we are going to get Indians into education and we're going to create better students, at some point the community is going to have to realize that education is the way that we are going to improve the state that we are in.... But I think it has to begin with educated leadership. And from there, you get good leaders, you got educated people making good decisions then that's going to help those kids out.... Maintaining the status quo in Indian communities to me is not acceptable.... And it can't be up to the federal government or the state government. It's got to be up to the tribal leadership. People that have a vested interest in the community.... People have to step into roles and take leadership and say things that some people might not want to hear or haven't heard before. Otherwise nothing is going to change, things will be the same. We've got a 47 percent dropout rate right now; we had a 50 percent dropout rate when I went to school. If nothing changes in the next fifteen years, half of these kids will not graduate. But I'm doing what I can and these kids see that. We have other good teachers

doing what they can. If we get enough good teachers, we get enough support, they will succeed.

The suggestion that schools should be used for cultural preservation is admittedly controversial. For a variety of reasons, there remains resistance to teaching cultural values and language in schools. For some tribes, many cultural elements (and even language) are so sacred that open discussion of these matters is regarded as inappropriate; some prefer tribal culture be taught privately within proper tribal relationships (Mondragón & Stapleton, 2005; Peshkin, 1997; Woodrum, 2009). Nevertheless, for many tribes schools may well be the most underused resource in the struggle to preserve tribal traditions and language. How ironic it would be if the institution of formal education, once a destructive force aligned against tribal cultures, ultimately proved itself as an instrument of cultural preservation for Native peoples. Virtually all of the educators I met believed schools should perform this function. A number were convinced schools will do so.

THE TIN MAN'S QUESTION

At the end of the movie *The Wizard of Oz,* after many adventures and misadventures, the Tin Man asks, "What have you learned, Dorothy?" It is a fair question to pose to anyone who has attempted research. Reflecting back on this investigative journey, I can say I have learned quite a lot: I gathered understanding on the unique strengths offered by differing types of Native educators. I gained insight on daunting challenges and precious rewards associated with serving reservation children. The educators I met led me to fuller understanding on the significance of cultural strengths for their students as well as for themselves.

Most important, I learned the value of hope in the professional and personal lives of a small number of American Indian educators serving a handful of distressed reservations in the Northern Plains of the United States. They toil away, invisible to virtually everyone outside their reservations. But the lack of public renown only adds to my admiration for their service. Society is filled with those who have gained an inordinate amount of public attention but seem to be famous merely for being famous. We find individuals who parlay a well-known family name combined with tantalizing online videos of their private lives as a means to garner notice. However, they have little to show in the way of talent or contribution as the reason for their celebrity. Ultimately, their impact on those charmed by the illusions of pop culture may be intense, but it is altogether fleeting. They will not be remembered or valued, because they give us nothing substantial to remember or value. The emperor has no clothes—and you can take that literally.

The Lakota word for children is *wakanyeja*. It literally means sacred beings. A whole philosophy of education (and of parenting) resides in the word *wakanyeja*. Children are considered the sacred ones because they are a gift from the Creator. Upon them rests the future of the tribe. Their care, their education, their future, is a sacred trust.

Those entrusted with the education of sacred beings have unique opportunities as well. The individuals I met during this research make significant and enduring contributions. They change lives. They expand possibilities. They preserve tribal culture. They offer hope for the future as well as for the present. These educators do give people something to remember and something to value. Consequently, they will be remembered and, although they may not always see it now, ultimately they will be valued by the people and the students they serve. They will be remembered and valued because they not only demonstrate hope, but also act on it. These American Indian educators, entrusted with the care of sacred beings, all deserve the name "Helps the People."

"What have you learned, Dorothy?" the Tin Man asks. I may not have traveled to Oz and I did not return to Kansas, but I did learn about Native educators who serve as beacons of hope in reservation schools.

APPENDIX

Methodology, Theoretical Framework, and Research with Native People

Research is a complex enterprise and requires much in the way of initial planning, actual execution, and eventual conclusion. This appendix provides an overview of three significant components of the research process behind this book. First, I outline the research methodology that structured the investigative process. Second, I discuss a critically important theoretical perspective known as transculturation theory that guided many of the issues I explored and that I used to assist with the explanations. Transculturation theory connects most directly with the material found in chapter 7. Third, I address crucial considerations about conducting research about American Indian peoples and Native communities.

METHODOLOGY

I employed an exploratory study using a conventional qualitative design with personal face-to-face interviews as a way to document the perceptions and experiences of a small sample of American Indian educators (Stebbins, 2001). Technically, I used the personal interviews within an ethnographic research framework in order to document the rich nuances typical of complex cultural perspectives and experiences (Fetterman, 2010). When used with personal interviews, ethnographies provide an effective means to understand how individuals create meaningful social actions within a specific cultural context (Spradley, 1979; Tedlock, 2000; Warren & Karner, 2005). Researchers often refer to these types of studies as microethnographies because they do not attempt to document the cultural patterns and life of a group of people over an extended period, as is common in the work of most cultural anthropologists (Fetterman, 2010; Ogbu, 1981). Rather, microethnographic studies aim to explore the perceptions and experiences among a small sample of individuals who share similar cultural experiences. Moreover, the objective of ethnographic research is to achieve theoretical insights either by examining existing theory or creating new theory (Erickson, 1977; Fetterman, 2010; Yon, 2003). The research process specifically consisted of four steps: gaining institutional approvals, sampling and contacting participants, conducting personal interviews, and analyzing the data.

A researcher must obtain permission before collecting data on an American Indian reservation. Not surprisingly, perhaps, gatekeepers played a critical role during the investigation. Navigating through all the necessary institutional levels took both time and effort. Throughout the research project, I kept a field journal (something like a researcher's diary) and recorded important events, tasks, and other notes essential for the effective completion of the investigation. The field journal provided an invaluable way to keep track of the necessary contacts and dates associated with institutional approvals.

After obtaining permission from my university's institutional review board (IRB), I turned to the appropriate tribal authorities for approval. Tribal governments differ in the procedures required to obtain permission for research. Some tribes have established formal IRBs, while others consider research applications through their tribal council, and still others refer such requests to the tribal education director. My request to conduct this investigation was considered and reviewed in all those ways. Tribal leaders are rightfully concerned with the nature of any research proposed for their reservation; in all cases, they carefully reviewed my application. In each request, I assured tribal authorities that none of the reservations would be identified in the reporting of the results. For that reason, throughout this book I refer to reservations only by their state location. I made this assurance not only to protect the identity of each reservation, but also as an added way to guard the anonymity of the participants located on reservations with only a few American Indian educators.

I made initial contact with a number of tribal chairs or tribal councils throughout the Northern Plains and Pacific Northwest and informed them of the nature and purpose of the research. Based on the response from each initial contact, I made a formal request to conduct research with the authorities of nine reservations located in Montana, Nebraska, Oregon, South Dakota, and Washington. I selected these reservations largely because they had in place some form of research review process. All but two of the reservations granted approval. One tribal IRB rejected the application due to the small number of American Indian educators on their reservation. Interestingly, the tribal IRB based their decision not on ethical, but rather methodological concerns. The IRB members felt that with only a few Native educators on the reservation, their participation would be little help to the research effort. In the other case, the tribal IRB disbanded before rendering a decision on my request. Unfortunately, the tribe did not install an alternative review process and the application was never acted upon.

Eventually, tribal authorities on seven reservations approved the research and granted me permission to collect data. I later discovered, however, there were no American Indian educators on one of the reservations while another reservation employed only one Native educator in its entire school system. Even though this lone educator wanted to participate in the research, the tribal IRB required a copy of all data collected from their reservation. This requirement would have compromised the lone educator's anonymity and confidentiality, and so I declined to interview that individual.

Ultimately, I had institutional permission and the realistic opportunity to conduct interviews on five reservations. Two of the reservations are located in Montana and the other three are in South Dakota. The next step involved contacting leaders of various school systems on those five reservations. This included contacting school superintendents and building principals. For the most part, simply having tribal approval for the research was sufficient for these individuals. I supplied all parties with information on the nature and purpose of the research and no one at the school system level declined to cooperate with the investigation.

The parameters required all participants be active educators (including teachers and administrators), American Indian, and currently serving in a reservation school. Unfortunately, the fact there are so few American Indian educators frustrated the research effort and simply identifying the Native educators from each of the five reservations proved challenging. In order to create a sampling list, I used a combination of purposive and snowball sampling techniques.

In a purposive sampling strategy, the researcher identifies participants based on characteristics considered of theoretical importance to the investigation (Bogdan & Biklen, 1992). My investigation specifically required a purposive sampling technique because of its focus on the experiences of American

Indian educators who serve in reservation schools. Thus, I developed an initial sampling list based on information gleaned from school websites and state American Indian education associations. Although I used this method to identify most of the educators eventually included on the sampling list, I needed to supplement the purposive sampling with a snowball sampling approach.

Snowball sampling is a rather simple procedure that is particularly useful when potential participants are difficult to locate (Berg, 2007; Lee, 1993). A researcher using snowball sampling simply asks key informants to identify individuals who have characteristics important to the investigation. Using the information provided by key informants, the researcher recruits individuals for the study and, thereby, grows his or her sample. I initiated the snowball sampling when I contacted school superintendents and principals. Thus, school superintendents and principals served as the key informants for this investigation. Because I had already identified most Native educators using purposive sampling techniques, only a few of the potential participants were invited to engage in the investigation based on information provided by superintendents and principals.

Using purposive and snowball sampling techniques, I assembled a sampling list of forty-five American Indian educators and contacted all of them with an invitation to participate in the research. Twenty-five out of the forty-five initially agreed to an interview. Unfortunately, scheduling conflicts and personal circumstances prevented the participation of four individuals and I ultimately interviewed only twenty-one of these educators. Eleven of the participants were from the two Montana reservations and ten were from the three South Dakota reservations. Although it took some effort and time to negotiate entrée to do the research and assemble a sampling list, generally the educators responded quickly and enthusiastically to the request for participation.

I conducted the personal interviews during the spring and fall of 2010. During those two trips, I traveled to the five reservations, interviewing educators and visiting nine different schools. Each participant selected the time and place for the interview; the locations included classrooms, staff meeting rooms, principals' offices, and restaurants. In one case, I even conducted an interview in the hallway while workers busily went about routine maintenance and cleaning as part of the end of the academic year.

During the interviews, I proceeded from an interview schedule consisting of guide questions while I simultaneously pursued important issues and experiences as they emerged. Researchers will recognize this technique as involving a semistructured interview approach (Roulston, 2010). In fact, I provided a copy of the guide questions to each participant before personally meeting for the face-to-face interview. I felt compelled to do this for several reasons. First, I was more interested in the considered reflections of the educators than on spontaneous responses to "surprise" questions. Second, this procedure had the added effect of allowing the participants to more fully understand the nature of the investigation and, thereby, of reducing any concerns over exploitative research—sadly an all-too-common occurrence in previous work with Native peoples (Swisher & Tippeconnic, 1999). I wanted the participants to see for themselves the interview questions were not only personally inoffensive, but also that they could potentially produce significant information for them, their schools, and their communities.

The interview schedule consisted of both general and specific questions structured around three components: the personal and cultural background of the participant; the participant's experience as an educator, including perceptions on NCLB and tribal culture; and the participant's professional goals. While interviewing, I noticed some questions generated rich information whereas a few questions did not produce particularly significant insights. As a result, during the course of interviewing I intentionally stressed the potentially more important questions by allowing for more time and using a greater number of probes while I placed less emphasis on questions generating weaker information. For example, the interview schedule included a guide question inquiring on the nature of the educator's college experience. I wanted to explore if any earlier cultural conflicts while in college might be related to the pathway into education or influence the participant's teaching experiences. Cultural conflict was not a major issue as many of the participants had attended local tribal colleges. Thus, it did not take too many interviews to discover that, to borrow from Gertrude Stein, there wasn't any there there. I continued to ask the question whenever appropriate to do so, but, given the limited amount of time with each participant, I chose not to keep probing an issue that appeared to produce little insight. On the other hand, it became clear the educators had a lot to say about their roles with students and the larger community. This part of the interview generated tremendously textured information, and I quickly became aware of the need to devote more interview time and use more probes with these questions.

With permission, I recorded the interviews and transcribed them myself. This procedure greatly aided the analysis by producing a heightened intimacy with the data. Moreover, I kept copious field notes on the general nature of the educators' experiences and perceptions and noted anything that might prove theoretically significant. The transcriptions of the interviews primarily and the field notes secondarily constitute the sources for the final data analysis and interpretation.

The data analysis included a three-stage process of initial coding, focused coding, and thematic coding (LeCompte & Schensul, 1999; Miles & Huberman, 1994). During initial coding, I sorted answers to each of the interview schedule questions (along with other extemporaneous questions) into tentative response categories using an in vivo technique in which a researcher uses the participants' own words to create a coding category. Thus, each specific response reflecting a sentiment, perception, or experience constituted an individual category. An in vivo technique is rather tedious but also very thorough.

Next, during focused coding I reviewed the initial coding categories in order to identify similarities among the responses (Auerbach & Silverstein, 2003). I collapsed individual responses into a smaller number of common response categories and subsequently reviewed the categories in order to evaluate if they should be further combined. I continued this procedure until satisfied I could no longer reasonably merge categories. At this point, I treated the finalized categories as themes. In effect, themes represent a shared perception or experience among the participants; I gave them labels for quick reference. Thus, my data analysis essentially involved a search for themes—recurring experiences and perceptions expressed by the participants I could describe in some detail and dignify with a label.

The last phase, thematic coding, involved two general procedures. First, I considered the themes for conceptual similarities. In essence, I asked whether any of the themes cluster together and appear to represent dimensions of a larger and more abstract theoretical notion. This consideration of the data led to the identification of a number of significant theoretical constructs. In my research, theoretical constructs are more abstract than specific themes. They act like a conceptual umbrella under which related themes group together. For instance, many of the participants discussed such specific challenges as ineffective educators or teacher turnover, and I considered them as themes. However, I understood the themes "ineffective educators" and "teacher turnover" are conceptually related to one other, so I created a theoretical construct called "school staff issues." Accordingly, I treated each of the specific themes as one of the dimensions of the larger theoretical construct. Second, I looked for connections between the themes. For instance, I wanted to know if specific self-defined roles the participants described are linked to particular challenges they identified.

Let me further illustrate the data analysis process with the interview question on the challenges related to serving in reservation schools. By using an in vivo approach, I found the participants offered sixty-eight specific responses to the question about challenges, so I created sixty-eight initial coding categories to the question. Obviously, the participants frequently used different words and expressions to describe essentially the same challenge. Thus, as part of focused coding I examined the sixty-eight categories for similarities and collapsed the categories as necessary. My intent was to create a smaller number of more meaningful themes. In this case, I created a theme only if seven—that is, one-third (an admittedly arbitrary threshold)—or more participants shared similar perceptions or experiences. The focused coding process resulted in thirteen themes on the challenges serving reservations schools. In thematic coding, I considered the thirteen themes for conceptual similarities. This led me to create four theoretical constructs. For instance, three of the specific themes—poverty, family dysfunctions, and alcohol and drug abuse—indicate challenges resulting from a larger, more abstract concept: the social conditions found on the reservations. As a result, I conceived the theoretical construct of reservation social conditions as including three dimensions (or themes) of specific challenges. Additionally, as part of thematic coding, I analyzed the theoretical constructs and corresponding themes for prevailing associations with other critical data. For instance, I considered whether the educators' perceived roles are linked to the types of challenges they identify.

The final part of the data analysis involved examining the themes and various relationships against the premise and assumptions of transculturation theory. Specifically, I attempted to gain an understanding of cultural identity issues by using the concept of transculturation as an a priori theme (Bernard & Ryan, 2010). An a priori theme is a theoretical concept a researcher believes he or she may discover because of the assumptions found in an existing theory. Essentially, I used the notion of transculturation as a sensitizing concept in order to discover if the participants identified cultural identity issues in the way suggested by transculturation theory.

THEORETICAL FRAMEWORK

Scholars developed transculturation theory specifically as a framework to explain the higher educational experiences of culturally oriented American Indian students. This theory is different from most theoretical perspectives in that it attempts to explain why American Indians are successful in college rather than why they fail (Huffman, 2010). Essentially, this theory maintains that culturally oriented American Indian students learn the cultural nuances found in mainstream higher education while retaining and relying on their cultural heritage to forge a strong identity and sense of purpose (Huffman, 2001; White Shield, 2009). Ultimately, one's cultural identity serves as a social psychological and cultural anchor enabling the culturally oriented individual to gain the confidence necessary to engage the mainstream institution without fear of cultural loss (Horse, 2005).

A key assumption of this framework is that individuals continually engage in cultural learning. Fundamentally, transculturation is a form of socialization, and in that regard is similar to the more commonly used concept of biculturation. However, there are significant conceptual differences between transculturation and biculturation. For instance, many scholars typically treat biculturation comparable to a mathematical equation in which an individual adds cultural elements from the dominant society, aligning those with cultural elements from his or her original cultural background while relinquishing unnecessary cultural ways (Garrett, 1996). Ultimately, biculturation assumes a sort of cultural hybrid end product. However, this typical conceptualization has been roundly criticized as little more than a variation of assimilation (see Henze & Vanett, 1993; O'Sullivan, 2007). Transculturation theory does not accept the notion cultural exchanges necessarily lead to cultural hybridization with resultant cultural loss. Rather, the reflective and rational individual can retain intact tribal cultural ways, views, and beliefs while learning those of a new culture. Ultimately, the transculturation process does not require an individual to relinquish former cultural ways to make room for new ones as implied in the usual conceptualization of biculturation (Huffman, 2008; Sill, 1967; White Shield, 2004).

Scholars have used transculturation theory almost exclusively within American Indian higher educational studies. However, I believed transculturation theory could provide a framework to understand the perceptions on student success among Native educators serving in reservation schools. Transculturation theory rests on the fundamental assertion that a strong cultural identity promotes effective participation in mainstream institutions. Operating from this premise, I wanted to examine if the participants would regard a strong cultural identity as essential for the academic and personal success of their students. Chapter 7 discusses how I explored this issue using the transculturation theoretical framework.

RESEARCH WITH NATIVE PEOPLES

The issue of research with Native peoples represents a thorny topic. Some object to social scientific methods and theories as culturally imperialistic. They represent conventional Western approaches to knowledge incapable of accurate descriptions of indigenous thought and values (Gobo, 2008). Others go so far as to contend only indigenous scholars should engage in scholarship on Native peoples and issues (Swisher & Tippeconnic, 1999). It is certainly difficult to counter these important protestations. Unfortunately, scholarship can result in the creation and perpetuation of stereotypes, faulty assumptions, and misguided policy. But scholarly investigations also produce numerous benefits, especially in education.

I take seriously the concerns regarding American Indian research. I am not a Native person and am quite aware I am a guest when doing research. Over the years, I have participated in research on American Indian issues under only two conditions: first, if invited to engage in research by a Native organization, and second, if I collaborate with a Native scholar. No tribal government or educational system first invited me to conduct this investigation. I initiated this research because I saw a need for the study based on the nature of the scholarly literature and from my personal experiences with Native educators. I also did not work specifically with an American Indian scholar as a coresearcher due to the timeframe and needs of my schedule.

Additionally, qualitative researchers must pay special attention to the issue of credibility. At the heart of their concerns is the question of validity. Researchers have developed a variety of validation strategies to increase the accuracy and integrity of their findings and interpretations (Creswell & Miller, 2000). I relied on a number of these strategies in an effort to enhance the accuracy of this research. First, I made every attempt to stay in the field long enough to gather sufficient data, and was sensitive to the need to achieve a satisfactory saturation point (Fetterman, 2010). Second, I utilized what Altheide and Johnson (1994) call "validity-as-reflexive-accounting" (p. 489), whereby the data are reviewed numerous times and in multiple ways in order to truly make sense of the patterns and themes emerging from the interviews. This technique does not allow for a superficial review of the data but a thorough examination, reexamination, and further reexamination (Patton, 1980). Third, I liberally employed verbatim quotations excerpted from the interviews as a means to convey the sentiments and experiences of the participants. This technique is a form of thick description (Fetterman, 2010).

Fourth, I used triangulation by engaging in personal interviews, direct observation, and analysis of field notes (Miles & Huberman, 1994). Fifth, I employed the expertise of an advisory committee consisting of five American Indian elementary or secondary educators and higher education scholars who served as an external audit (Creswell, 2007; Lincoln & Guba, 1985). These individuals come from a variety of tribal, disciplinary, and professional backgrounds, but all have expertise in American Indian education. Most notable among the functions of the advisory committee included advising on the general research approach, reviewing and modifying the guide questions for the personal interviews, and providing insight into and perspective on the findings, interpretations, and conclusions of the research.

Regrettably, I did not use participant checking of the findings and interpretations (Creswell, 2007). In hindsight, this validation technique would have likely added to the strength and credibility of the findings. The absence of this measure represents a shortcoming of the research endeavor.

References

Altheide, D., & Johnson, J. (1994). Criteria for assessing interpretive validity in qualitative research. In N. K. Denzin & Y. S. Lincoln (Eds.), *Handbook of qualitative research* (pp. 485–499). Thousand Oaks, CA: Sage.

Altshuler, S., & Schmautz, T. (2006). No Hispanic student left behind: The consequences of "high-stakes" testing. *Children & Schools, 28*(1), 5–14.

Ambler, M. (1999). Instilling dreams: The promise of teacher education. *Tribal College Journal, 11*(2), 6–9.

Ambler, M. (2006). School reform requires local involvement. *Tribal College Journal, 17*(4), 8.

Auerbach, C., & Silverstein, L. (2003). *Qualitative data: An introduction to coding and analysis.* New York: New York University Press.

Ballou, D., & Podgarsky, M. (1995). Rural schools—fewer highly trained teachers and special programs, but better learning environment. *Rural Development Perspectives, 10*(3), 6–16.

Balter, A., & Grossman, F. (2009). The effects of the No Child Left Behind Act on language and culture education in Navajo public schools. *Journal of American Indian Education, 48*(3), 19–46.

Beaulieu, D. (2008). Native American education research and policy development in an era of No Child Left Behind: Native language and culture during the administrations of presidents Clinton and Bush. *Journal of American Indian Education, 47*(1), 10–45.

Beaulieu, D., & Figueira, A. (Eds.). (2006). *The power of Native teachers: Language and culture in the classroom.* Tempe: Center for Indian Education, Arizona State University.

Beesley, A., Atwill, K., Blair, P., & Barley, Z. (2010). Strategies for recruitment and retention of secondary teachers in central U.S. rural schools. *The Rural Educator, 31*(2), 1–9.

Begaye, T. (2007). Native teacher understanding of culture as a concept for curricular inclusion. *Wicazo Sa Review, 22*(1), 35–52.

Berg, B. (2007). *Qualitative research methods for the social sciences* (6th ed.). Boston: Allyn & Bacon.

Bergstrom, A. (2009). *Ji-AAnjichigeyang "to change the way we do things": Retention of American Indian students in teacher education* (Unpublished doctoral dissertation). University of Minnesota, St. Paul.

Berman, M. (2002). Alcohol control policies and American Indian communities. In P. Mail, S. Heurtin-Roberts, S. Martin, & J. Howard (Eds.), *Alcohol use among*

American Indians and Alaska Natives: Multiple perspectives on a complex problem (pp. 87–109), Bethesda, MD: National Institute on Alcohol Abuse and Alcoholism.

Bernard, H. R., & Ryan, G. W. (2010). *Analyzing qualitative data: Systematic approaches.* Thousand Oaks, CA: Sage.

Beynon, J. (2008). *First Nations teachers: Identity and community, struggle and change.* Calgary, AB: Detselig.

Bogdan, R., & Biklen, S. (1992). *Qualitative research for education: An introduction to theory and methods.* Needham Heights, MA: Allyn & Bacon.

Boyer, P. (2006). It takes a Native community. *Tribal College Journal, 17*(4), 14–19.

Brown, C., Gibbons, J., & Eretzian Smirles, K. (2007). Tribal teachers are important to American Indian adolescents' tribal identity development. *American Indian Culture and Research Journal, 31*(2), 103–111.

Brunetti, G. J. (2001). Why do they teach? A study of job satisfaction among high school teachers. *Teacher Education Quarterly, 28*(3), 49–74.

Byrd-Blake, M., Afolayan, M., Hunt, J., Fabunmi, M., Pryor, B., & Leander, R. (2010). Morale of teachers in high poverty schools: A post-NCLB mixed methods analysis. *Education and Urban Society, 42*(2), 450–472.

Cajete, G. (2006). It is time for Indian people to define indigenous education on our own terms. *Tribal College Journal, 18*(2), 56–57.

Chavers, D. (2000). Indian teachers and school improvement. *Journal of American Indian Education, 39*(2), 49–59.

Cherubini, L. (2008). New aboriginal teachers' experiences: An undiscovered landscape. *Canadian Journal of Native Education, 31*(2), 34–50.

Cherubini, L., Kitchen, J., & Trudeau, L. (2009). Having the spirit within to vision: New aboriginal teachers' commitment to reclaiming space. *Canadian Journal of Native Education, 32*(2), 38–51.

Cherubini, L., Niemczyk, E., Hodson, J., & McGean, S. (2010). A grounded theory of new aboriginal teachers' perceptions: The cultural attributions of Medicine Wheel teachings. *Teachers and Teaching: Theory and Practice, 16*(5), 545–557.

Cockburn, A. D. (2000). Elementary teachers' needs: Issues of retention and recruitment. *Teaching and Teaching Education, 16*(2), 223–238.

Coladarci, T. (1983). High-school dropouts among Native Americans. *Journal of American Indian Education, 23*(1), 15–22.

Cookson, P. (2005). Why teach? *Teaching PreK–8, 36*(3), 14–16.

Cornell, S., & Kalt, J. P. (2000). Where's the glue?: Institutional and cultural foundations of American Indian economic development. *Journal of Socio-Economics, 29*(5), 443–470.

Creswell, J. (2007). *Qualitative inquiry and design: Choosing among five traditions* (2nd ed.). Thousand Oaks, CA: Sage.

Creswell, J., & Miller, D. (2000). Determining validity in qualitative inquiry. *Theory into Practice, 39*(3), 124–130.

Cummins, J. (2007). Pedagogies for the poor? Realigning reading instruction for low-income students with scientifically based reading research. *Educational Researcher, 36*(9), 564–572.

Darling-Hammond, L. (2003). Keeping good teachers: Why it matters, what leaders can do. *Educational Leadership, 60*(8), 6–13.

Darling-Hammond, L. (2007). Evaluating "No Child Left Behind." *The Nation, 284*(20), 11–18.

Davis, S. (1986). The participant of Indian and Metis parents in the school system. *Canadian Journal of Native Education, 13*(2), 32–39.

Deloria, V., & Wildcat, D. (2001). *Power and place: Indian education in America*. Boulder, CO: Fulcrum Resources.

Dessoff, A. (2010). Persuading teachers to go rural. *District Administration, 46*(6), 58–62.

Deyhle, D. (1992). Constructing failure and maintaining cultural identity: Navajo and Ute school leavers. *Journal of American Indian Education, 31*(2), 24–47.

Dingman, S., Mroczka, M., & Brady, J. (1995). Predicting academic success for American Indian students. *Journal of American Indian Education, 34*(2), 10–17.

Duquette, C. (2002). Becoming a teacher: Experiences of First Nations student teachers in isolated communities. *Canadian Journal of Native Education, 24*(2), 134–143.

Elliott, D., Menard, S., Rankin, B., Elliot, A., Wison, W., & Huizinga, D. (2006). *Good kids from bad neighborhoods: Successful development in social context*. New York: Cambridge University Press.

Eppley, K. (2009). Rural schools and the highly qualified teacher provision of No Child Left Behind: A critical policy analysis. *Journal of Research in Rural Education, 24*(4). http://jrre.psu.edu/articles/24-4.pdf.

Epstein, J. (2001). *School, family, and community partnerships: Preparing educators and improving schools*. Boulder, CO: Westview Press.

Erickson, F. (1977). Some approaches to inquiry in school-community ethnography. *Anthropology & Education Quarterly, 8*(2), 59–69.

Erickson, J. L., Terhune, M. N., & Ruff, W. G. (2008). Measuring work conditions for teachers of American Indian students. *Researcher, 21*(2), 1–10.

Fetterman, D. M. (2010). *Ethnography: Step-by-step* (3rd ed.). Thousand Oaks, CA: Sage.

Figueira, A. (2006). The Native educators research project. In D. Beaulieu & A. Figueira (Eds.), *The power of Native teachers: Language and culture in the classroom* (pp. 7–61). Tempe: Center for Indian Education, Arizona State University.

Forbes, J. (2000). The new assimilation movement: Standards, tests, and Anglo-American supremacy. *Journal of American Indian Education, 39*(2), 7–28.

Forte, E. (2010). Examining the assumptions underlying the NCLB federal accountability policy on school improvement. *Educational Psychologist, 45*(2), 76–88.

Fox, S. J. (1999). Student assessment in Indian education, or what is a roach? In

K. Swisher & J. Tippeconnic (Eds.), *Next steps: Research and practice to advance Indian education* (pp. 161–178).

Friese, B., Grube, J., Seninger, S., Paschall, M., & Moore, R. (2011). Drinking behavior and sources of alcohol: Differences between Native American and white youths. *Journal of Studies on Alcohol and Drugs, 72*(1), 53–60.

Friesen, D., & Orr, J. (1998). New paths, old ways: Exploring the places of influence on the role identity. *Canadian Journal of Native Education, 22*(1), 188–200.

Froelich, K., & Medearis, C. (1999). Sitting Bull's vision: A collaboration that works for our children. *Tribal College Journal of American Indian Higher Education, 11*(2), 18–20.

Garcia, D. (2008). Mixed messages: American Indian achievement before and since the implementation of No Child Left Behind. *Journal of American Indian Education, 47*(3), 136–154.

Garrett, M. (1996). "Two people": An American Indian narrative of bicultural identity. *Journal of American Indian Education, 36*(1), 1–21.

Garrett, M., Bellon-Harn, M., Torres-Rivera, E., Garrett, J., & Roberts, L. (2003). Open hands, open hearts: Working with Native youth in the schools. *Intervention in School and Clinic, 38*(4), 225–235.

Gobo, G. (2008). *Doing ethnography.* Thousand Oaks, CA: Sage.

Grande, S. (2004). *Red pedagogy: Native American social and political thought.* Lanham, MD: Rowman & Littlefield.

Granovetter, M. (1973). The strength of weak ties. *American Journal of Sociology, 78*(6), 1360–1380.

Gustafson, J. M. (1982). Professions as callings. *The Social Service Review, 56*(4), 501–515.

Hansen, D. T. (1994). Teaching and the sense of vocation. *Educational Theory, 44*(3), 259–276.

Hardy, L. (2005). A place apart. *American School Board Journal, 192*(4), 18–23.

Hargreaves, A., & Shirley, D. (2008). Beyond standardization: Powerful new principles for improvement. *Phi Delta Kappa, 90*(2), 135–143.

HeavyRunner, I., & DeCelles, R. (2002). Family education model: Meeting the student retention challenge. *Journal of American Indian Education, 41*(2), 29–37.

Henze, R. C., & Vanett, L. (1993). To walk in two worlds—or more?: Challenging a common metaphor of Native education. *Anthropology and Education Quarterly, 24*(2), 116–134.

Hess, F. M. (2008). When education research matters. *Society, 45*(6), 534–539.

Hill, B., Vaughn, C., & Brooks-Harrison, S. (1995). Living and working in two worlds: Case studies of five American Indian women teachers. *The Clearing House, 69*(1), 42–49.

Hill, D., & Barth, M. (2004). NCLB and teacher retention: Who will turn out the lights? *Education and the Law, 16*(2–3), 173–181.

Hood, S. (1998). Culturally responsive performance-based assessment: Conceptual and psychometric considerations. *Journal of Negro Education, 67*(1), 187–199.

Horse, P. G. (2005). Native American identity. *New Directions for Student Services, 109*(1), 61–68.

Huffman, T. (2001). Resistance theory and the transculturation hypothesis as explanations of college attrition and persistence among culturally traditional American Indian students. *Journal of American Indian Education, 40*(3), 1–23.

Huffman, T. (2005, November). *Academic achievement through cultural autonomy: Enhancing higher educational persistence for culturally traditional American Indians.* Paper presented at the meeting of the People of Color in Predominately White Institutions Conference, Lincoln, NE.

Huffman, T. (2008). *American Indian higher educational experiences: Cultural visions and personal journeys.* New York: Peter Lang.

Huffman, T. (2010). *Theoretical perspectives on American Indian education: A new look at educational success and the achievement gap.* Lanham, MD: AltaMira Press.

Ingalls, L., Hammond, H., Dupoux, E., & Baeza, R. (2006). Teachers' cultural knowledge and understanding of American Indian students and families: Impact of culture on a child's learning. *Rural Special Education Quarterly, 25*(1), 16–24.

Jennings, J. (2011). The policy and politics of rewriting the nation's main education law. *Phi Delta Kappa, 92*(4), 44–49.

Johnson, J., & Strange, M. (2007). *Why rural matters 2007: The realities of rural education growth.* Arlington, VA: Rural School and Community Trust.

Jones, M. G., Jones, B. D., & Hargrove, T. (2003). *The unintended consequences of high-stakes testing.* Lanham, MD: Rowman & Littlefield.

Juneau, D., & Smoker Broaddus, M. (2006). And still the waters flow: The legacy of Indian education in Montana. *Phi Delta Kappa, 88*(3), 193–197.

Kawagley, A. (1999). Alaska Native education: History and adaptation in the new millennium. *Journal of American Indian Education, 39*(1), 31–51.

Kelting-Gibson, L. (2006). Preparing educators to meet the challenges of Indian Education for all. *Phi Delta Kappa, 88*(3), 204–207.

Klug, B., & Whitfield, P. (2003). *Widening the circle: Culturally relevant pedagogy for American Indian children.* New York: Routledge Falmer.

Kovas, A., McFarland, B., Landen, M., Lopez, A., & May, P. (2008). Survey of American Indian alcohol statutes, 1975–2006: Evolving needs and future opportunities for tribal health. *Journal of Studies on Alcohol and Drugs, 33*(3), 183–191.

Lamb, C. (2010). Turtle Mountain teachers train change agents. *Tribal College Journal, 22*(2), 40–41.

LeCompte, M. D., & Schensul, J. J. (1999). *Analyzing and interpreting ethnographic data.* Walnut Creek, CA: AltaMira Press.

Lee, R. M. (1993). *Doing research on sensitive topics.* Thousand Oaks, CA: Sage.

Lieberman, A., & Miller, L. (1992). *Teachers, their world and their work: Implications for school improvement.* New York: Teachers College Press.

Lieberman, A., & Miller, L. (1999). *Teachers—transforming their world and their work.* New York: Teachers College Press.

Liesveld, R., Miller, J. A., & Robison, J. (2005). *Teach from your strengths: How great teachers inspire their students.* New York: Gallup Press.

Lincoln, Y. S., & Guba, E. G. (1985). *Naturalistic inquiry.* Newbury Park, CA: Sage.

Linn, R., Baker, E., & Betebenner, D. (2002). Accountability systems: Implications of requirements of the No Child Left Behind Act of 2001. *Educational Researcher, 31*(6), 3–16.

Lipka, J., & Mohatt, G. (1998). *Transforming the culture of schools: Yu'ik Eskimo examples.* Mahwah, NJ: Lawrence Erlbaum.

Lomawaima, K. T., & McCarty, T. (2006). *"To remain an Indian": Lessons in democracy from a century of Native American education.* New York: Teachers College Press.

Lonczak, H., Fernandez, A., Austin, L., Marlatt, G. A., & Donovan, D. (2007). Family structure and substance use among American Indian youth: A preliminary study. *Families, Systems, & Health, 25*(1), 1–22.

Mainor, P. (2001). Family matters: Fort Peck Community College tests holistic approach to student success. *Tribal College Journal, 12*(4), 10–13.

Manuelito, K. (2003). *Building a Native teaching force: Important considerations* (ERIC Document Reproduction Service No. ED482324).

McCarty, T. (2008). American Indian, Alaska Native, and Native Hawaiian education in the era of standardization and NCLB—An introduction. *Journal of American Indian Education, 47*(1), 1–9.

McGuinn, P. J. (2006). *No Child Left Behind and the transformation of federal education policy, 1965–2005.* Lawrence: University Press of Kansas.

McKenna, M., & Walpole, S. (2010). Planning and evaluating change at scale: Lessons from Reading First. *Educational Researcher, 39*(6), 478–483.

Miles, M. B., & Huberman, M. A. (1994). *Qualitative data analysis: An expanded sourcebook* (2nd ed.). Thousand Oaks, CA: Sage.

Miller Cleary, L., & Peacock, T. D. (1998). *Collected wisdom: American Indian education.* Needham Heights, MA: Allyn & Bacon.

Mills, C. W. (1959). *The sociological imagination.* New York: Oxford University Press.

Mitchem, K., Kossar, K., & Ludlow, B. (2006). Finite resources, increasing demands: Rural children left behind? Educators speak out on issues facing rural special education. *Rural Special Education Quarterly, 25*(3), 13–23.

Mondragón, J., & Stapleton, E. (2005). *Public education in New Mexico.* Albuquerque: University of New Mexico Press.

Monk, D. (2007). Recruiting and retaining high-quality teachers in rural areas. *The Future of Children, 17*(1), 155–174.

Mullany, B., Barlow, A., Goklish, N., Larzelere-Hinton, F., Cwik, M., Craig, M., &

Walkup, J. (2009). Toward understanding suicide among youths: Results from the White Mountain Apache tribally mandated suicide surveillance system, 2001–2006. *American Journal of Public Health, 99*(10), 1840–1848.

Nelson-Barber, S., & Trumbull, E. (2007). Making assessment practices valid for indigenous American students. *Journal of American Indian Education, 46*(3), 132–147.

Ngai, P., & Koehn, P. (2010). Implementing Montana's Indian Education for All initiative in a K–5 public school: Implications for classroom teaching, educational policy, and Native communities. *Journal of American Indian Education, 49*(1/2), 50–68.

Noguera, P. (2010). A new vision for school reform: The change we need in education policy. *The Nation, 290*(23), 11–14.

Ogbu, J. (1981). School ethnography: A multilevel approach. *Anthropology & Education Quarterly, 12*(1), 3–29.

Osterholm, K., Horn, D., & Johnson, W. (2006). Finders keepers: Recruiting and retaining teachers in rural schools. *National Forum of Teacher Journal, 17*(3), 1–12.

O'Sullivan, D. (2007). *Beyond biculturalism: The politics of an indigenous minority.* Wellington, NZ: Huia.

Palmer, P. (2007). *The courage to teach: Exploring the inner landscape of a teacher's life.* San Francisco: John Wiley & Sons.

Patton, M. Q. (1980). *Qualitative evaluation methods.* Newbury Park, CA: Sage.

Pavel, M., Banks, S. R., & Pavel, S. (2002). The Osale story: Training teachers for schools serving American Indians and Alaska Natives. *Journal of American Indian Education, 41*(2), 38–47.

Peacock, T. (2006). Native students speak: What makes a good teacher? *Tribal College Journal, 17*(4), 10–13.

Pearson, L. C., & Moomaw, W. (2005). The relationship between teacher autonomy and stress, work satisfaction, empowerment, and professionalism. *Educational Research Quarterly, 29*(1), 37–53.

Pem, M. (2010). Fighting the suicide spirit. *Diverse: Issues in Higher Education, 27*(21), 14–15.

Pember, M. A. (2007). A mandate for Native history. *Diverse: Issues in Higher Education, 24*(7), 18–19.

Perrachione, B. A., Rosser, V. J., & Petersen, G. J. (2008). Why do they stay? Elementary teachers' perceptions of job satisfaction and retention. *Professional Educator, 32*(2), 25–41.

Peshkin, A. (1997). *Places of memory: Whiteman's schools and Native American communities.* New York: Routledge.

Pewewardy, C. (2002). Learning styles of American Indian/Alaska Native students: A review of the literature and implications for practice. *Journal of American Indian Education, 41*(3), 22–56.

Philips, S. (1983). *The invisible culture: Communication and community on the Warm Spring reservation.* New York: Longman.

Phillips, M. (2006). Standardized tests aren't like T-shirts: One size doesn't fit all. *Multicultural Education, 14*(1), 52–55.

Powers, K. (2006). An exploratory study of cultural identity and culture-based educational programs for urban American Indian students. *Urban Education, 41*(1), 20–49.

Ravitch, D. (2010). *The death and life of the great American school system: How testing and choice are undermining education.* New York: Basic Books.

Reyhner, J. (1992). American Indians out of school: A review of school-based causes and solutions. *Journal of American Indian Education, 31*(2), 37–56.

Reyhner, J., & Eder, J. (2004). *American Indian education: A history.* Norman: University of Oklahoma Press.

Reyhner, J., & Hurtado, D. (2008). Reading First, literacy, and American Indian/Alaska Native students. *Journal of American Indian Education, 47*(1), 82–95.

Rhodes, R. (1994). *Nurturing learning in Native American students.* Hotevilla, AZ: Sonwai Books.

Robertson, P., Jorgensen, M., & Garrow, C. (2004). Indigenizing evaluation research: How Lakota methodologies are helping "raise the tipi" in the Oglala Sioux nation. *American Indian Quarterly, 28*(3&4), 499–526.

Robinson-Zanartu, C., & Majel-Dixon, J. (1996). Parent voices: American Indian relationships with schools. *Journal of American Indian Education, 36*(1), 33–54.

Roulston, K. (2010). *Reflective interviewing: A guide to theory and practice.* Thousand Oaks, CA: Sage.

Rumbaugh Whitesell, N., Mitchell, C., & Spicer, P. (2009). A longitudinal study of self-esteem, cultural identity, and academic success among American Indian adolescents. *Cultural Diversity and Ethnic Minority Psychology, 15*(1), 38–50.

Scott, W. J. (1986). Attachment of Indian culture and the "difficult situation": A study of American Indian college students. *Youth & Society, 17*(4), 381–395.

Sill, M. L. (1967). Transculturation in four not-so-easy steps. In R. Hoopes (Ed.), *The Peace Corps experience* (pp. 246–267). New York: Clarkson N. Potter.

Skinner, L. (1999). Teaching through traditions: Incorporating languages and culture into curricula. In K. Swisher & J. Tippeconnic (Eds.), *Next steps: Research and practice to advance Indian educator* (pp. 107–134). Charleston, WV: ERIC Clearinghouse on Rural Education and Small Schools.

Smith-Davis, M. (2002). Teacher retention and small rural school districts in Montana. *The Rural Educator, 24*(2), 45–52.

Spradley, J. (1979). *The ethnographic interview.* New York: Holt, Rinehart and Winston.

Stebbins, R. (2001). *Exploratory research in the social sciences.* Thousand Oaks, CA: Sage.

Swisher, K., & Tippeconnic, J. (Eds.). (1999). *Next steps: Research and practice to advance Indian education.* Charleston, WV: ERIC Clearinghouse on Rural Education and Small Schools.

Tedlock, B. (2000). Ethnography and ethnographic representation. In N. K. Denzin & Y. S. Lincoln (Eds.), *Handbook of qualitative research* (2nd ed.), (pp. 455–486). Thousand Oaks, CA: Sage.

Tickle, B. R., Chang, M., & Kim, S. (2011). Administrative support and its mediating effect on U.S. public school teachers. *Teaching & Teacher Education, 27*(2), 342–349.

Tienken, C. H. (2011). Common core standards: The emperor has no clothes, or evidence. *Kappa Delta Pi, 47*(2), 58–62.

Tippeconnic, J., & Faircloth, S. (2006). School reform, student success for educators working with Native K-12 students. *Tribal College Journal, 17*(4), 26–29.

Vadas, R. (1995). Assessing the relationship between academic performance and attachment to Navajo culture. *Journal of Navajo Education, 12*(2), 16–25.

Van Hamme, L. (1996). American Indian cultures and the classroom. *Journal of American Indian Education, 35*(2), 21–34.

Villegas, C. (2006, August). *Raising red Atlantis: Path dependence and the ironies of the Native American reservation system, 1887–2005*. Paper presented at the annual meeting of the American Sociological Association, Montreal, QC.

Ward, C. (2005). *Native Americans in the school system: Family, community, and academic achievement.* Lanham, MD: AltaMira Press.

Warren, C., & Karner, T. (2005). *Discovering qualitative methods: Field research, interviews, and analysis.* Los Angeles: Roxbury.

Whitbeck, L., Hoyt, D., Stubben, J., & LaFromboise, T. (2001). Traditional culture and academic success among American Indian children in the Upper Midwest. *Journal of American Indian Education, 40*(2), 48–60.

White Shield, R. (2004). The retention of indigenous students in higher education: Historical issues, federal policy, and indigenous resilience. *Journal of College Student Retention, 6*(1), 111–127.

White Shield, R. (2009). Identifying and understanding indigenous cultural and spiritual strengths in the higher education experiences of indigenous women. *Wicazo Sa Review, 24*(1), 47–63.

Wilkinson, C. (2005). *Blood struggle: The rise of modern Indian nations.* New York: W. W. Norton.

Willeto, A. A. A. (2007). Native American kids: American Indian children's well-being indicators for the nation and two states. *Social Indicators Research, 83*(1), 149–176.

Williams, R., Massaro, T., Airhart, P., & Zikmund, B. (2004). The teacher's career and life. *Teaching Theology and Religion, 7*(4), 181–200.

Willmon-Haque, S., & BigFoot, D. S. (2008). Violence and the effects of trauma on American Indian and Alaska Native populations. *Journal of Emotional Abuse, 8*(1/2), 51–66.

Winstead, T., Lawrence, A., Brantmeier, E., & Frey, C. (2008). Language, sovereignty, cultural contestation, and American Indian schools: No Child Left Behind and a Navajo test case. *Journal of American Indian Education, 47*(1), 46–64.

Woodrum, A. (2009). Cultural identity and schooling in rural New Mexico. *Journal of Research in Rural Education, 24*(8). http://jrre.psu.edu/articles/24-8.pdf.

Yon, D. A. (2003). Highlights and overview of the history of educational ethnography. *Annual Review of Anthropology, 32*(1), 411–429.

Yu, M., & Stiffman, A. (2007). Culture and environment as predictors of alcohol abuse/dependence symptoms in American Indian youths. *Addictive Behaviors, 32*(10), 2253–2259.

Yu, M., & Stiffman, A. (2010). Positive family relationships and religious affiliation as mediators between negative environment and illicit drug symptoms in American Indian adolescents. *Addictive Behaviors, 35*(7), 694–699.

Zehr, M. A. (2007). Varied strategies sought for Native American students. *Education Week, 27*(5), 8.

Zost, G. (2010). An examination of resiliency in rural special educators. *The Rural Educator, 31*(2), 10–14.

Index

adequate yearly progress (AYP), 72, 95, 96, 99, 100, 104, 106–10, 145, 146
affinitive educators, 9, 10, 14–20, 23–34, 36–38, 41, 47, 50–52, 55–60, 63–65, 67–69, 71–75, 80, 82, 84–90, 92, 95, 99, 101, 104–10, 115, 116, 119, 121, 122, 125, 127, 133, 135–40, 143–46; definition of, 15
affirming rewards, 80–85, 89, 90, 144, 145; definition of, 80
African American, 133
Airhart, Phyllis, 12
Alaska Native, 91, 97
alcoholism, 54, 55, 58, 62, 67, 70, 75, 108, 114, 158. *See also* substance abuse
Altheide, David, 160
altruistic rewards, 80, 85–90, 144, 145; definition of, 85
Altshuler, Sandra, 103
Ambler, Marjane, 4, 16, 128, 149
America, 1, 100, 111, 114. *See also* United States
assimilation, 5, 39, 40, 63, 115, 142, 159
attrition (student), 77
Atwill, Kim, 149
Auerbach, Carl, 157
Austin, Lisette, 59

Baeza, Rosalinda, 97
Baker, Eva, 106
Ballou, D., 4, 91
Balter, Allison, 97, 105
Banks, Susan Rae, 13
Barley, Zoe, 149
Barth, Marlene, 47
Barzun, Jacques, 79
Beaulieu, David, 4, 124

Beesely, Andrea, 149
Begaye, Timothy, 31, 126
Belcourt, North Dakota, 33
Bellon-Harn, Monica, 128
Berg, Bruce, 155
Bergstrom, Amy, 5
Berman, Matthew, 59
Bernard, H. Russell, 158
Betebenner, Damian, 106
Beynon, June, 4, 13
bicultural, 39, 114, 159
BigFoot, Dolores, 69
Biklen, Sari, 154
Blair, Pamela, 149
boarding school(s), 60, 77, 82, 100
Bogan, Robert, 154
Boyer, Paul, 4, 128, 149
Brady, James, 128
Brantmeier, Edward, 98
Brooks-Harrison, Shannon, 6
Brown, Carrie, 142
Brunetti, Gerald T., 76
Bureau of Indian Affairs, 101
Bureau of Indian Education, 122
Bush administration, 106
Byrd-Blake, Maria, 108

Cajete, Gregory, 4, 128
California, 78, 111
Canadian First Nations, 13, 31
Carlisle Indian School, 60
challenges (in teaching American Indian students), ix, x, 2, 4, 5, 6, 10, 53–77, 79, 80, 91, 92, 105, 131, 143, 144, 150, 157, 158. *See also* core challenges; peripheral challenges
Chang, Mido, 76

Chavers, Dean, 4, 13, 16, 119, 128
Cherubini, Lorenzo, 6, 13, 120
child abuse and neglect, 54, 57, 58, 61, 114
Cockburn, Anne D., 76
Coladarci, Theodore, 77, 128
community development, 64, 86, 90
Congress, 96, 101, 106
Cookson, Peter, 89, 92
core challenges, 75, 76, 144; definition of, 75
Cornell, Stephen, 4
credibility (of qualitative research), 160. *See also* validity
Creswell, John, 160, 161
cultural conflict, 156
culturally relevant education, 4, 20, 22, 34, 105, 114, 129, 136, 137, 140, 146, 148
cultural/tribal identity, ix, 5, 13, 40, 64, 125–27, 129, 131–36, 139–42, 146–48; ambiguity and, 133–35, 146, 158, 159
cultural/tribal preservation, 4, 13, 21, 26, 30–32, 64, 80, 85, 87–89, 93, 112, 128, 129, 136–38, 140, 146, 148–51
cultural/tribal traditions, 2, 9, 13, 24–26, 28, 30, 31, 34, 39, 40, 50, 78, 93, 110, 114, 115, 127, 128, 132–35, 137, 138, 141, 148–50; rejection of, 133, 134, 156
Cummins, Jim, 97

Dakota, 125
Darling-Hammond, Linda, 76, 111
Davis, Sidney, 20
DeCelles, Richard, 21
definitional roles, 15
Deloria, Vine, 4
Dessoff, Alan, 47, 49
Deyhle, Donna, 5
Dingman, Sherry, 128
direct path (into education), 40, 41, 43, 51, 146; definition of, 40–41
domestic violence, 27, 54, 57. *See also* family dysfunctions

Donovan, Dennis, 59
Dr. Seuss, 111
drug abuse, 55, 58, 62, 67, 75, 108, 114, 158. *See also* substance abuse
Dupoux, Errol, 97
Duquette, Cheryll, 14, 31, 126

Eder, Jeanne, 5
Elliott, Delbert, 16
Epply, Karen, 47
Epstein, Joyce, 32
Eretzian Smirles, Kimberly, 142
Erickson, Joanne L., ix, x, 4, 6, 47, 74, 77, 153

facilitative educators, 9, 10, 14, 15, 19, 22–30, 32–34, 36–38, 41, 47, 50–52, 55–60, 64, 65, 67–75, 80, 82, 84–90, 95, 99, 101, 104, 105, 107–10, 115–17, 119, 121, 122, 127, 133, 135–40, 143–46; definition of, 22
Faircloth, Susan, 128
family dysfunctions, 20, 55, 57, 58, 61, 63, 70, 75, 83, 99, 108, 144, 158
Fernandez, Anne, 59
Fetterman, David M., 152, 153, 160
Figueira, Anna, 4, 124
Forbes, Jack, 4, 96, 98, 101, 115
Forte, Ellen, 96, 107
foundational roles, 15, 30; definition of, 30
Fox, S. J., 128
Frey, Christopher, 98
Friese, Bettina, 59
Friesen, David, 14
Froelich, K., 124

Garcia, David, 98
Garrett, J. T., 128
Garrett, Michael, 128, 159
Garrow, Carrie, 4
Gibbons, Judith, 142

Gobo, Giampietro, 160
Grande, Sandy, 128
Granovetter, Mark, 122
Grossman, Frank, 97, 105
Grube, Joel, 59
Guba, Egon E., 161
Gustafson, James M., 12

Hammond, Helen, 97
Hansen, David, 12
Hardy, Lawrence, 74
Hargreaves, Andy, 108
Hargrove, Tracy, 96
Head Start, 131
HeavyRunner, Iris, 21
Henze, Rosemary, 159
Hess, Frederick M., 4
Hill, Brenda, 6, 13
Hill, Deborah, 47
Hodson, John, 13
Hood, Stafford, 103
Horn, Deborah, 4
Horse, Perry, 159
Hoyt, Dan, 141
Huberman, Michael A., 157, 161
Huffman, Terry, 64, 141, 142, 159
Hurtado, Denny, 97

Indian Education for All, 100, 110, 138, 140
Indian Health Service, 9
indirect path (into education), 40, 41, 43, 46, 47, 51; definition of, 41
Ingalls, Lawrence, 97
institutional review board (IRB), 153, 154

Jennings, Jack, 111
Johnson, Jerry, 91
Johnson, John, 160
Johnson, Wanda, 4
Jones, Brett D., 96
Jones, M. Gail, 96, 97

Jorgensen, Miriam, 4
Juneau, Denise, 110

Kalt, Joseph P., 4
Kansas, 151
Karner, Tracy, 152
Kawagley, Angayuqau, 119
Kelting-Gibson, Lynn, 110
Kim, Sunha, 76
Kitchen, Julian, 13
Klug, Beverly, 4, 128
Koehn, Peter, 110
Kossar, Kalie, 107
Kovas, Anne, 59

LaCompte, Margaret D., 157
LaFromboise, Teresa, 141
Lakota, 22, 151
Lamb, Carmelita, 33, 34, 128
Landen, Michael, 59
Lawrence, Adrea, 98
Lee, Raymond M., 155
Lieberman, Ann, 2, 13, 28–30, 32, 33, 90, 91
Liesveld, Rosanne, 12
Lincoln, Yvonna S., 161
Linn, Robert, 106
Lipka, Jerry, 5, 119
Lomawaima, K. Tsianina, 4, 5
Lonczak, Heather, 59
Lopez, Adriana, 59
Ludlow, Barbara, 107

Mainor, Peggy, 21
mainstream cultural orientation, 36–39, 51, 52, 89, 141
mainstream culture/society, 4, 98, 132, 137, 148, 159
Majel-Dixon, Juanita, 20, 77
Manuelito, Kathryn, 120, 124
Marlatt, G. Alan, 59
Maslow's hierarchy, 17, 56

Massaro, Thomas, 12
May, Philip, 59
McCarty, Teresa, 4, 5, 96–98
McFarland, Bentson, 59
McGean, Sarah, 13
McGinn, Patrick J., 4
McKenna, Michael, 97
Medearis, C., 124
Miles, Matthew B., 157, 161
Miller, Dana, 160
Miller, George, 111
Miller, Jo Ann, 12
Miller, Lynne, 2, 13, 28–30, 32, 33, 90, 91
Miller Cleary, Linda, 4, 6, 52, 119, 120, 128, 142, 148
Mills, C. Wright, 113
Missoula, Montana, 88
Mitchell, Christina, 141
Mitchem, Katherine, 107
Mohatt, Gerald, 5, 119
Mondragón, Joe, 150
Monk, David, 91
Montana, 7, 9, 11, 16–28, 30, 32, 35, 38–43, 45, 46, 48, 53, 55–63, 65–67, 69–73, 78, 79–84, 86–88, 94, 99–102, 104, 105, 107, 110, 111, 113–20, 123, 125, 128, 133–35, 137, 138, 140, 141, 149, 153–55
Moomaw, William, 76
Moore, Roland, 59
Mroczka, Mary, 128
Mullany, Britta, 69

Native American studies, 39, 83, 137
Native Hawaiian, 97
Navajo, 105, 140
Nebraska, 153
Nelson-Barber, Sharon, 103, 106
New Mexico, 77
Ngai, Phyllis, 110
Niemczyk, Ewelina, 13

No Child Left Behind (NCLB), ix, 2, 5, 10, 47, 72, 94–98, 100–112, 131, 145, 146, 156
Noguera, Pedro, 111
North Dakota State University, 121
Northern Plains, 1, 2, 21, 150, 153
Northwest Indian College, 91

Obama, President, 95
Ogbu, John, 153
Oregon, ix, 153
Orr, Jeff, 14
Osterholm, Karen, 4
O'Sullivan, Dominic, 159

Pacific Northwest, 153
Palmer, Parker, 13
Paschall, Mallie, 59
Patton, Michael Q., 160
Pavel, Michael, 13, 91, 128
Pavel, Susan, 13
Payne, Rudy, 62
Peacock, Thomas, 4, 6, 52, 115, 119, 120, 128, 142, 148
Pearson, L. Carolyn, 76
Pem, Mary, 69
Pember, Mary A., 110
peripheral challenges, 75, 76, 144; definition of, 76
Perrachione, Beverly A., 76
Peshkin, Alan, 5, 77, 128, 141, 150
Petersen, George T., 76
Pewewardy, Cornel, 142
Philips, Susan, 20
Phillips, Michele, 4
Podgarsky, M., 4, 91
poverty, 20, 54, 55–58, 61, 62, 73–75, 81, 99, 107, 108, 144, 158
Powers, Kristin, 141, 147
powwow, 84, 135. *See also* wacipi
Pueblo, 77

Quality of Life Teacher Work Life Survey, ix

Race to the Top, 95
racism, 20, 71, 73–76, 144; reverse racism, 141
Ravitch, Diane, 4, 96, 111
Reading First, 97
retention (teacher), 43, 47–50, 69, 74, 76, 91, 120
rewards (in teaching American Indian students), ix, x, 2, 4–6, 10, 77–93, 131, 143–45, 150. *See also* affirming rewards; altruistic rewards
Reyhner, Jon, 5, 97, 128
Rhodes, Robert, 52
Roberts, Lisen, 128
Robertson, Paul, 4
Robinson-Zanartu, Carol, 20, 77
Robison, Jennifer, 12
roles (self-defined by educators), x, 2, 4, 5, 13–34, 36, 43, 51, 143, 158. *See also* definitional roles; foundational roles
Rosser, Vicki T., 76
Roulston, Kathryn, 156
Ruff, William G., ix
Rumbaugh Whitesell, Nancy, 141
Ryan, Gery W., 158

Schensul, Jean J., 157
Schmautz, Tresa, 103
Scot, Wilbur, 142
self-confidence, 18, 45, 66, 123. *See also* self-esteem
self-esteem, 26, 140. *See also* self-confidence
Seninger, Steve, 59
Shirley, Dennis, 108
Sill, Maurice, 159
Silverstein, Louise, 157
Sitting Bull, 125
Skinner, Linda, 148
Smith-Davis, M., 91
Smoker Broaddus, Marty, 110
Sociological Imagination, The, 113
Solla Sollew, 111
South Dakota, 1, 3, 7, 13, 17, 18, 21, 23–27, 31, 37, 41–46, 48, 56–58, 60, 65–68, 71–73, 79–87, 92, 94, 102, 104, 107, 110–12, 116–23, 125, 130, 133, 134, 137–40, 153–55
South Dakota State University, 121
Spicer, Paul, 141
Spradley, James, 152
standardized tests and testing, 4, 5, 94–107, 109, 110, 115, 145, 146
standards (educational), 96, 97, 106, 110
Stapleton, Ernest, 150
Stebbins, Robert, 152
Stein, Gertrude, 156
Stiffman, Arlene, 58, 59
Strange, Marty, 91
Stubben, Jerry, 141
substance abuse, 54. *See also* alcoholism; drug abuse
suicide, 36, 47, 54, 64, 67–69, 76, 100, 114, 139
Sun Dance, 39
Swisher, Karen, 4, 119, 124, 156, 160

Tedlock, Barbara, 152
Terhune, M. Neil, ix
Tickle, Benjamin R., 76
Tienken, C. H., 96
Tippeconnic, John, 4, 119, 124, 128, 156, 160
Title III, 104
Title IV, 104
Torres-Rivera, Edil, 128
transculturation theory, 5, 10, 131–33, 135, 136, 140, 142, 146–48, 152, 158, 159

tribal college(s), 39, 43, 45–47, 51, 120, 121, 124, 128, 149
tribal cultural education, 95, 97, 98, 100, 103–6, 109–12, 117, 129–32, 136–40, 142, 145–47, 148
tribal cultural orientation, 36–39, 51, 52, 85, 88, 92, 110, 125, 127, 135, 139, 141, 146, 147, 159
Trudeau, Lyn, 13
Trumbull, Elise, 103, 106
Turtle Mountain Community College, 33

United States, 4, 69, 150. *See also* America
University of Montana, 41

Vadas, Robert, 140
validity (of qualitative research), 160, 161; validation strategies, 160, 161. *See also* credibility
Vanett, Lauren, 159
Van Hamme, Linda, 101
Vaughn, Courtney, 6
Villegas, C., 4

wacipi, 84. *See also* powwow
wakanyeja, 151

Walpole, Sharon, 97
Ward, Carol, 5, 47
War on Poverty, 111
Warren, Carol, 152
Washington, 154
Washington State University, 91
Whitbeck, Les, 141, 147
White Shield, Rosemary, 126, 159
Whitfield, Patricia, 4, 128
Wilcox, Colleen, 12
Wildcat, Daniel, 4
Wilkinson, Charles, 77
Willeto, A. A. A., 58, 59
Williams, Raymond, 12
Willmon-Haque, Sadie, 69
Winstead, Teresa, 98
Wizard of Oz, The, 150
Woodrum, Arlie, 128, 150
Wyoming, 130

Yon, Daniel, 153
Yu, ManSoo, 58, 59

Zehr, Mary Ann, 107, 148
Zikmund, Barbara, 12
Zost, Gregory, 91